MiG 'Killer', Maj Rankin in aerial combat flying No. 3 Squadron Mirage F.1CZ over Angola, on 6 November 1981. (Illustration from painting of event, by ex-SAAF W.O. Tiro Vorster).

Rear Cover:
Indigenous Atlas CSH-2 Rooivalk attack helicopter.

Air Force Insignia:
Far right: WWII aircraft marking. Blue circle, white background, orange centre
Other: No. 1 Squadron. SAAF premier squadron. 'Prima'

— Contents —

The Squadron Badges of the SAAF
Illustrations & line drawings
Photographs

1. Unie van Suid Afrika (Union of South Africa) Air Force

2. New Equipment

3. Bush Wars

4. The Helicopters

5. The 'new' SAAF

6. '75' in Ninety-Five

7. Very Important Base's

8. South African Police Air Wing

APPENDIX   I: South African Air Force (SAAF) Equipment Circa 2003/4
APPENDIX II: SAAF Battle Order — Circa 2003
APPENDIX III: SAAF Indigenous Aircraft Names, Markings, Codes and Serials.
APPENDIX IV: ATLAS AVIATION, A Division of DENEL (Pty) Ltd.
APPENDIX V: C-47TP Turbo-Daks
APPENDIX VI: SAAF Museum Airplane Inventory

Bibliography & Sources
Acknowledgements

Squadron Badges of the South African Airforce

South Africa

No. 28 Squadron 50th
Anniversary Hercules
(ad astra)

1 Squadron	2 Squadron	3 Squadron	4 Squadron	5 Squadron
First	Upward and onward	Always fighting	Death to the enemy	We shall confront all difficulties

6 Squadron	7 Squadron	SQUADRON BADGES OF THE SAAF	8 Squadron
Beware	Lords of the skies		Until death

11 Squadron	12 Squadron		15 Squadron
Let courage not fail	First into battle		The eagle seeks the heights

16 Squadron	17 Squadron	19 Squadron	21 Squadron	22 Squadron
Attack	As the occasion arises	Fame from deeds	Unbeatable	That the sea may be free

24 Squadron	**25 Squadron**	**27 Squadron**	**28 Squadron**	**35 Squadron**
Through night, through day	We help	We protect	We carry	Strike at the water
40 Squadron	**41 Squadron**			**42 Squadron**
The eye of the army	We find the enemy			

The Silver Falcons (Afrikaans name: *Die Silwer Valke*) aerobatic team comprises some of the finest pilots in the SAAF; all are instructors at the Flying Training School at Langebaanweg. At the time of writing, the Silver Falcons fly standard Impala trainers which bear consecutive numbers on their tailfins.

				CFS
				Our deeds will live
FTS	**AFS 85**	**AFS 86**	**AFS 87**	**AFS 88**
Holding fast to my purpose, I conquer	Our purpose is damage	We teach flying	We teach	We teach the guardians of the shores

1. Unie van Suid Afrika (Union of South Africa) Air Force

In 1913, six South African Army officers of the Union Defence Forces, had received flying training at a flying school at Kimberley, later being sent to join the Royal Flying Corps in the UK for further training. Even so, at the outbreak of WW I in 1914, there was no air arm to support the Union Defence Force and in 1915, the South African Aviation Corp (SAAC) was founded under Major Van der Spuy. Initial equipment consisted of ex-Royal Naval Air Service (RNAS) Henri Farmans and BE.2as and in May 1915, reconnaissance sorties began to be flown by the SAAC to German-West Africa in support of the South African Army engaged in removing German forces from the area. Two months later the German colony surrendered.

SAAC personnel were now sent to the UK where in October 1915, they became No. 26 'South African' Squadron of the Royal Flying Corps equipped with Henri Farman F.27 and Royal Aircraft Factory B.E.2s. The squadron left for East Africa in December 1915, arriving in Mombasa on 31 January, 1916. German forces based in Tanganyika posed a threat to British East Africa and No.26 Squadron had been sent to assist Imperial forces in dispersing the enemy and to occupy the German East African colonies. From August 1917, the squadron used only B.E.2c and B.E.2e airplanes in East Africa. In February 1918, the need for the squadron had diminished, and in June it returned to the UK via Cape Town, and having been redesignated No.26 Squadron RAF en-route, it disbanded at Blandford Camp, on 8 July 1918. The force having fought with distinction in East Africa, where the Germans were generally superior in numbers, with technically superior airplanes, including Rumplers and a few Fokkers.

Authorisation to form the Suid -Afrikaanse Lugmag /South African Air Force (SAAF) was given on the 1 February 1920, when Colonel Pierre Van Ryneveld was appointed Director of Air Services. Recruiting began in June 1920, the basis of the new air arm formed by the squadron that had served with the Royal Flying Corps (RFC) during the First World War. The new air force was established in April 1921, with 113 donated airplanes, most comprising the "Imperial Gift" of one hundred ex-RAF aircraft provided by the British Government, including twenty-two S.E.5A fighters, forty-eight Airco D.H.4/D.H.9 and D.H. 9A bombers and thirty Avro 504K trainers. Supplemented by a further donation of ten D.H. 4s and a single D.H. 9 to form a composite training unit, No.1 Flight at Swartkop, leading to the establishment of the first Flying Training School the following year. The air arm also included a reserve, the Active Citizen Defence Force. During the early years the force was involved mainly in policing duties, flying an airmail service between Durban and Cape Town, along with surveying, and training duties of Citizen Defence Force pilots.

In 1929 Avro Avian trainers were purchased to replace the 504Ks, while thirty-one Westland Wapati general-purpose biplanes were also placed in service plus a further twenty-seven assembled locally at the Artillery Depot, Roberts Heights. In the 1930s fifty-seven Avro Tutors were licence-built there.

When the Suid-Afrikaanse Lugmag was established in April 1921, with 113 airplanes donated by the British Government. Its first fighters were twenty-one ex-WWI RAF S.E. 5A

SE5A cockpit

A major expansion programme was started in 1936. Sixty-five Hawker Hart bombers were manufactured under licence as the Hartebees, while equipment supplied direct from the United Kingdom included Hawker Fury and Hawker Hurricanes and Gloster Gladiator fighters, Fairey Battle and Bristol Blenheim bombers. A steady flow of obsolescent ex-RAF Hawker Harts, Hinds and Demon biplanes arrived from the UK to equip training schools. Even so, only 104 combat aircraft were in service at the outbreak of World War II in September 1939. In addition 18 Junkers Ju 86 airliners of South African Airways (SAA) were pressed into service on maritime-reconnaissance duties. Later, its 11 Junkers Ju 52's were formed into a Bomber Transport Brigade and, with the Ju 86's, formed part of a SAAF unit which participated in the Abyssinian campaign. In June, 1940, SAA ceased all civil operations and 28 Lockheed Lodestars, which had been ordered in 1940, were also incorporated in the SAAF and, together with the Ju 52s were used on military transport services throughout Africa.

In January, 1944, Colonel Leverton, who had commanded the Bomber Transport Brigade, resumed his duties as Acting Manager of South African Airways and ten Lodestars were eventually made available for the resumption of scheduled air services on 1 December, 1944.

At the time Britain declared war on Germany, in 1939, it was not absolutely certain if South Africa would join the Allies as there was a sizeable portion of the population in sympathy with Fascism. Nevertheless, within days of the invasion of Poland, the Union joined the rest of the Commonwealth in the war against Germany. At first all SAAF operational units were engaged on coastal patrols around the Cape. At the same time, although South Africa was not part of the Empire Flying Training Scheme, SAAF training facilities were greatly expanded and placed at the disposal of the RAF to form the Joint Air Training Scheme (JATS). At its peak the JATS had thirty-three schools and over 30,000 men were trained during the war, about 27 per cent being for the SAAF. By February 1944, a total of about 16,000 aircrews including 5,000 pilots, a similar number of observers, 2,000 navigators, 2,000 bomb aimers and 2,000 air gunners had been trained in the Union. The majority of aircrews then received their operational training at RAF schools established in the Middle East.

Throughout the war the SAAF operated maritime reconnaissance patrols in the South Atlantic and Indian Ocean, while other units fought in the Western Desert in North Africa against Italian and German forces, eventually liberating Ethiopia, and in Europe after taking part in the Allied invasion of Sicily. The entry of Italy into the war in June 1940, brought a major threat from Italian East Africa to the Sudan and Kenya. But, at this stage of the war, troops and airplanes to counter a new enemy were in short supply. SAAF units were immediately hurried north to Kenya, with a mixed collection of airplanes. The former South African Airways converted Junkers Ju-86 formed the heavy bomber force, indigenous Hartbees formed the army co-operation element, while a small force of Hawker Fury IIs and six Gloster Gladiator biplanes equipped the fighter squadrons.

Locally-built armoured Hawker Hartbees were used to good effect in Kenya against the Italians early in WWII
(Hawker Aircraft Ltd)

The southern front in Kenya became the premise of the SAAF while the RAF supported British and Indian Army units defending the Sudan. It is all credit to the SAAF that after some initial successful Italian actions, both Allied armies moved into Ethopia, Italian Somaliland and Eritrea and by April 1941 enemy resistance had been reduced to such a state whereby SAAF units could be redeployed to the Middle East. Re-equipping with British Hawker Hurricanes, American Curtiss P-40 Mohawks and Martin Maryland bombers and later Curtiss Tomahawk fighters supplied to Egypt.

At home in South Africa, Bristol Beaufort torpedo-bombers and Lockheed Ventura supplemented Avro Ansons on coastal patrol duties which extended up through East Africa. Curtiss Mohawk fighters provided air defence, especially after Japan entered the war, as there was a strong possibility a Japanese task force would attack ports on the Indian Ocean. SAAF units also supported the occupation of Madagascar to deny the island to the Japanese.

In the Western Desert SAAF fighter and bomber units formed an integral part of the Desert Air Force and were active throughout the successful campaign to clear the enemy from Africa. When the Axis forces surrendered in May 1943, the SAAF had seven fighter and fighter-reconnaissance, three bomber, one photographic reconnaissance and two maritime patrol squadrons available for duties in the Mediterranean. Unfortunately as most SAAF personnel had been recruited for service in Africa, many expressed their reluctance to venture further afield and before any SAAF units could accompany the Desert Air Force to Sicily and Italy, volunteers had to be called for. It is of interest that almost all of the aircrew opted to go to Europe but replacements had to be recruited for many of the ground staff. On arrival in Italy the SAAF provided air support for the Eighth Army. Two heavy bomber squadrons were formed and other SAAF squadrons moved up from the Union to undertake anti-submarine patrols in the Mediterranean, with one other patrolling off West Africa.

Martin B-26 Marauders were operational with SAAF bomber squadrons from 1943 onwards. It was a demanding airplane to fly, but in the hands of an experienced pilot, it was a formidable weapon.

Squadrons of the SAAF continued to operate throughout 1944, with the Royal Air Force in the Middle East, Mediterranean, in Italy and the Balkans. Many squadrons served with the First Tactical Air Force of the RAF and in addition SAAF squadrons shared in the defence and patrolling of the Mediterranean from Alexandria to Algiers, and of the seas off West Africa to Cape Town, and the Indian coast from Cape Point to the Red Sea. A number of these units equipped with Lockheed Venturas were part of the Coastal Air Defence Arm stationed in the Union working in co-operation with RAF Catalina squadrons.

SAAF squadrons were involved in all the major Allied operations undertaken in the Italian theatre until the successful conclusion of that campaign in May, 1945. They were equipped with Consolidated Liberator heavy bombers, Martin Marauder and Baltimore medium bombers, rocket-firing Bristol Beaufighters, Curtiss Kittyhawk and Supermarine Spitfire fighters and North American P-51 fighter-bombers. The premier Marauder Wing of the SAAF had flown more than 21,000 operational sorties against the enemy up to the end of 1944. A number of SAAF crews were seconded to the RAF to fly Liberator and Wellington bombers.

One Spitfire squadron completed its 2,000th operation, which also included its 7,224th wartime sortie, early in 1945. Spitfires of another SAAF squadron were responsible for photographing the Germans' defence system in the Central Sector of the Hitler Line in Italy before the start of the Allied offensive in May, 1944. During May 1944, SAAF Spitfire fighter-bombers in Italy flew a record number of sorties attacking and damaging railway lines 129 times and dropping 400 tons of bombs on major communication centres. On three occasions special messages of congratulation from the Army were received by the SAAF. In addition, medium bombers and rocket-firing Bristol Beaufighter torpedo-bombers of the SAAF, achieved many successes in strikes against enemy shipping in the Aegean Sea.

In addition to direct support of Army operations in Italy throughout the year, squadrons of the SAAF served with the Balkan Air Force in support of Marshall Tito's forces in Yugoslavia. In addition South Africans flying Liberators were involved in flying supplies to Polands capital, Warsaw, during the Patriot rising there in the summer of 1944. A SAAF transport squadron equipped with Douglas C-47 Dakotas and operating with a Mediterranean Group under the auspices of RAF Transport Command completed more than one million miles flying during 1944 and carried five million pounds of air freight and mail, including 13,000 passengers. A shuttle service was operated by SAAF transport planes between Pretoria and Rome. The service flown in six days. By the end of 1944, a total of 40,000 passengers, 779,000 lbs of mail and 1,734,000 lb of freight had been carried along this route the airplanes flying a total of more than 9.5 million miles.

The veritable Douglas C-47 has served the SAAF well, both in WWII and post-war.

As a diversion in August 1944, a number of troop transports flown by the SAAF shared in the movement of new recruits for the South African 6th Division from Pretoria to a base in the Middle East where they were to complete their training. The operation involved the crews and airplanes in more than 4,000 miles flying. In addition to these operations in the Mediterranean and the Middle East other South African airmen served throughout the year with the RAF in all commands and in all theatres. The only South African seconded to the RAF's Bomber Command Pathfinder Force, Captain Edwin Swales DFC was posthumously awarded the Victoria Cross for his actions during a raid on a German communications centre on the night of 23 February 1945. Master Bomber Swales flying an Avro Lancaster of No. 582 Squadron (RAF) continued his attack over Pforzheim, 20 miles south-east of Karlsruh, whilst continuing to broadcast instructions to the main force despite two attacks by night fighters which holed fuel tanks and put out of action two engines and the rear turret. Almost defenceless, he stayed over the target area issuing his aiming instructions until he was satisfied that the attack had achieved its purpose. Subsequently it became known that the raid was one of the most concentrated and successful of the war.

On the return flight turbulent conditions and its slow speed made the damaged Lancaster almost uncontrollable and once over friendly territory, realising the situation was critical, Captain Swales ordered his crew to abandon the bomber, as it became more and more difficult to control. The bomber, by now was losing height steadily, time was very short and it required all Swales exertions to keep the airplane steady while each of the crew moved in turn to the escape hatch and parachuted to safety. Hardly had the last crew-member left the aircraft, sacrificing his own chances to escape, still struggling to keep it as steady as possible the bomber plunged to earth. Captain Swales was found dead at the controls.

The famous Avro Lancaster heavy bomber as flown by Master Bomber Captain Edwin Swales V.C., DFC.
(example, No. 44 (B) Squadron (RAF) the first unit to fly the type in 1942.)

Throughout World War II, the SAAF operated all the then current American and British military types available. At the end of the War the force was singled out for comment by Air Chief Marshal Tedder (RAF) for its notable contribution to victory...

SAAF major operational activities during WW II are related in the succeeding brief squadron histories. Much of its organisation was similar to the RAF, on which it was originally modelled. The *Suid-Afrikaanse Lugmag* / South African Air Force title reflects the dual White languages of the Republic of South Africa: Afrikaans, a variant of Dutch, and English. Squadron numbering beginning at No.1 commenced in February, 1920. Squadrons retained their number and badge from the time of formation and have not undergone any re-numbering when moved from base to base or on disbandment and reformation. In major contrast to its wartime cousin, the RAF.

No.1 Squadron was officially formed in February 1940, with Major N. G. Niblock-Stuart as the first Commanding Officer. Initially the squadron moved to Kenya in May 1940, as a fighter squadron equipped with Hawker Fury and Gloster Gladiator biplanes and later with Hawker Hurricanes. In November 1940, No.1 Squadron flew a defensive patrol of ten Gladiators (6 SAAF and 4 RAF) over Metemma but were "jumped" by a formation of Fiat CR 42s of the *Regia Aeronautica,* flown by battle hardened Italian pilots that had learnt their trade in the Spanish Civil War. However, this was only the first phase of the East African campaign and even though this was not the only Italian success, the SAAF despite losses, more than held its own against Mussolini's air force. In fact there can be no doubt that with the introduction of the Hawker Hurricane to its inventory, in spite of its numerical superiority, the SAAF dealt the *Regia Aeronautica* a severe blow in the campaign, from which it never fully recovered.

As resistance faded in Italian East Africa, No.1 was sent north to join the RAF's fighter force in Egypt.

Equipped with Hawker Hurricane IIBs the squadron arrived in Egypt on 16 April 1941, to operate over the Western Desert on escort and interception duties but in December 1941, No.1 Squadron began flying ground-attack missions against enemy targets in Libya. Re-equipping with Hurricane IIC in September 1942, excepting for brief breaks in the fighting the squadron remained in action until it converted to Supermarine Spitfire Mk VCs in November, 1942.

After the Battle of Alamein No.1 Squadron moved forward through Libya to Tunisia providing bomber escorts as well as undertaking offensive sweeps over enemy-held territory. At the end of the North African campaign in June 1943, it moved to Luqa, Malta to cover the Allied landings in Sicily. Moving to Italy in September 1943, the squadron provided support for Field Marshal Montgomery's Eighth Army operations. In recognition of the valuable air support it provided for the troops, Montgomery granted the unit the right to use the Crusader Cross in its emblem. The unit gained many battle honours during the war, its combat successes amounting to 165.5 "kills", 26 probables, another 130 damaged during aerial combat and more than 60 enemy airplanes were destroyed on the ground. The unit claiming more air combat victories than any other SAAF squadron. As the war ended the squadron was already converting to North American P-51 Mustangs but only a few were received before its personnel left for South Africa on 12 July, 1945, and demobilisation until reformed again in 1946, at Waterkloof Air Base near Pretoria. In 2003, No.1 'Prima' Squadron formed part of the SAAF's 'modern' 21st Century battle order equipped with Mirage F.1AZ ground-attack planes at Hoedspruit AFB.

No.1 Squadron WW II Equipment: *Hawker Fury, Gloster Gladiator. 1940 - Apr 41; Hawker Hurricane IIB, Apr 41 - Sep 42; Hurricane IIC, Sep 42 - Nov 42.Supermarine Spitfire VC, Nov 42 - Sep 43*; Spitfire VIII, Aug 43 - Oct 43*, Nov 43 - Jun 45. Supermarine Spitfire IX, June 43 - Aug 43*, Sep 43 - Oct 43. North American P-51 Mustang, Jun 45 - Jul 45.*
Note: British Air Ministry wartime unit Identification Code 'AX' carried for periods indicated *.

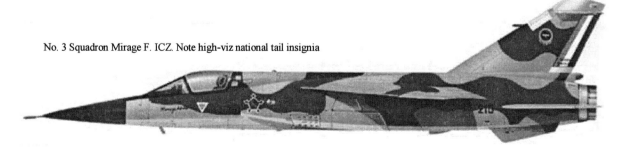

No. 3 Squadron Mirage F. ICZ. Note high-viz national tail insignia

8

F/sgt D Rowles

Mirage F.1 in its semi-hardened shelter. Note undernose laser range finder *(ad astra)*.

No. 2 Squadron Atlas Cheetah D on dispersal at Louis Trichardt AB *(ad astra)*.

No.2 (Transvaal) Squadron formed in January 1939, at Waterkloof AB and was deployed to the Middle East in the early stages of WW II. It arrived at Sidi Haneish in Egypt during July 1941, having previously operated Hawker Fury and Gloster Gladiator biplanes and Hawker Hurricane monoplane fighters in Kenya. Until September 1941, it trained on Curtiss Tomahawks before commencing offensive sweeps over the Western Desert.

In April 1942, the squadron began to re-equip with Kittyhawks initally for bomber escort duties and fighter sweeps until increasing numbers of Supermarine Spitfires equipping the Desert Air Force took over the escort duties. No.2 Squadron SAAF became increasingly involved in ground-attack duties in support of the Eighth Army during its advance through Libya after the Battle of El Alamein. During the final months of the North African campaign the unit was engaged in fighter-bomber raids in the battle area, attacking enemy communications, bases and airfields in Tunisia.

On converting to Supermarine Spitfire VCs the squadron moved to Sicily in July 1943, becoming operational again on 23 August. The following month it moved into newly-captured airfields in Italy initally to provide fighter cover for the Allied armies, until lack of enemy air activity, permitted a return to ground-attack duties for the rest of the war. A few North American Mustangs were received in June 1945, but on 12 July 1945 the squadron personnel left for South Africa. In 2003, No.2 Squadron formed part of the SAAF's 'modern' battle order equipped with Atlas Cheetah C multi-role fighters at Louis Trichardt AFB. No.2 Squadron's Training Flight operates Cheetah D dual-seat airplanes.

No.2 Squadron WW II equipment: *Curtiss Tomahawk IIB, Jul 41 - May 42; Curtiss Kittyhawk I, Apr 42 - Jun 43*; Kittyhawk III, Jun 43 - Jul 43. Supermarine Spitfire VC, Jul 43 - Mar 44; Spitfire IX, Feb 44 - Jul 45; North American P-51 Mustang Jun 45 - Jul 45.* Note: British Air Ministry wartime unit Identification Code 'DB' carried for periods indicated *.

No. 2 Squadron Atlas Cheetah C with centre-line fuel tank and low-viz markings *(ad astra).*

No.3 Squadron arrived at Suez, Egypt on 1 January 1943, direct from South Africa where it had reformed after completion of two years of operations in East Africa with Gloster Gladiator, Curtiss Mohawks and Hawker Hurricane fighters. Following a raid on Diredawa on 15 March 1941, the squadron claimed 10 enemy airplanes destroyed, and eight damaged, for two Hurricanes lost. In a most amazing feat of bravery one pilot Capt. J. Frost DFC who had already shot down two of the enemy aircraft when his own plane was hit and its engine seized, was rescued from his forced landing on an enemy satellite airfield, by his colleague Lt. R. H. C. Kershaw. Kershaw piloting another Hurricane witnessed Frost's demise and immediately set down through a barrage of enemy fire close to where he had landed. Frost climbed on to Kershaw's lap and in that position the two airmen flew back to base, with Frost operating the "stick" and rudder while Kershaw operated the "flap" and the undercarriage levers. For the brave recovery of his colleague Kershaw received the DSO, the first to be won by a South African in the war.

Almost immediately on arrival in Egypt No.3 Squadrons air crew transferred to RAF Khormaksar, Aden, to take over the Hawker Hurricane 1s of the Fighter Defence Flight. On returning to Egypt in mid-April 1943, eight of the Hurricanes were based at Helwan and on 23 April the units pilots took over thirteen Hurricane IICs from No.7 Squadron SAAF, but with the arrival of its ground echelon at Bersis in early May the airplanes were handed back to No.7 Squadron and No.3 Squadron received a full complement of Hawker Hurricane IIBs to fly shipping patrols along the Libyan coast. Conversion to Supermarine Spitfire Mk IXs in February 1944, saw a change to high-altitude interception duties, although re-equipment with Mk V Spitfires in March saw a resumption of normal tasks in support of the ground forces. At the end of July 1944, the squadron redeployed to Italy and the ground echelon was based at Bari, while its aircraft and pilots were attached to No.8 (SAAF) Wing. In August the unit re-equipped with Spitfire Mk IXs again and for the rest of the war it was engaged in ground-attack sweeps in support of the Allied Eighth Army.

The squadron remained in Italy until early September 1945, when many personnel began to move back to Egypt, its airplanes moving to Fayid at the end of the month. The squadron disbanded in theatre on 7 October 1945. No.3 Squadron was not included in the 'modern' battle order.

No.3 Squadron WW II equipment: *Hawker Hurricane 1, Jan 43 - Apr 43; Hurricane IIB, May 43 - Feb 44; Hurricane IIC, Nov 43 - Mar 44. Supermarine Spitfire VC, Mar 44 - Aug 44; Spitfire IX, Feb 44 - Oct 45.*

No. 3 Squadron flew Hawker Hurricanes until re-equipping with Spitfires in March 1944.
(example, No. 249 'Gold Coast' Squadron RAF).

No.4 Squadron was formed at Waterkloof on 25 March 1941, and deployed to Kenya as a fighter unit with Hawker Fury biplanes and Curtiss Mohawk monoplane fighters. On 1 September 1941, it left for Egypt and assembled at Amriya by the middle of the month to receive Curtiss Tomahawk becoming operational in November. Bomber escort and fighter sweeps over the Western Desert kept the squadron busy until June 1942, when it was withdrawn to re-equip with Curtiss Kittyhawks to resume operations at the end of the month. During and after the Battle of El Alamein, No. 4 Squadron flew fighter-bomber missions in support of the Eighth Army and supported the Allied troops during the clearance of Axis forces from Tunisia.

In July 1943, the squadron re-equipped with British Supermarine Spitfire VBs which were taken to Sicily early in August that year, the ground crews arriving on the 18th of the month. In September the squadron moved to Italy where it remained for the rest of the war, to fly ground-attack missions in support of the Allied armies in the battle area. Having re-equipped with Spitfire IXs in May 1944, on the 12 July 1945, the units personnel returned to South Africa. No.4 Squadron was not included in the 'modern' battle order.

No.4 Squadron WW II equipment: *Curtiss Tomahawk IIB, Oct 41 - Jun 42; Curtiss Kittyhawk I, Jun 42 - Jul 43* Supermarine Spitfire VB, Jul 43 - May 44*; Supermarine Spitfire IX, May 44 - Jul 45*.* Note: British Air Ministry wartime unit Identification Code 'KJ' carried for periods indicated *.

No.5 Squadron formed at Zwartkop on 7 May 1941, as a fighter unit with Curtiss Mohawks and left for Egypt in December that year. Various ground echelons were spread around Egypt while the units pilots underwent operational training in the Sudan with No. 71 Operational Training Unit (RAF) based at Ismailia, Egypt. Early in February 1942, the squadron reformed as a complete unit with Curtiss Tomahawk IIB and began bomber escort missions and fighter sweeps over the Western Desert. In June it had to retire to Egypt as its Libyan bases were over-run by the enemy and it remained there until November 1942. Re-equipping with Kittyhawks in January 1943, it then moved forward through Libya in support of the Eighth Army. Flying fighter-bomber sweeps behind the enemy lines, it hit communication centres and supply dumps while close support was provided for the army in attacks on enemy positions holding up the advance. After the clearance of the enemy from North Africa the squadron remained in theatre until August 1943, when it moved to Sicily to cover the Allied invasion of Italy. In mid-September, it occupied captured airfields on the mainland and it remained in Italy for the rest of the war to fly fighter-bomber missions in support of the Allied troops.

Operations with Kittyhawks ceased on 26 September 1944, and resumed on 3 October when north American P-51 Mustangs were received. Mustangs were subsequently flown on fighter sweeps over Italy and Yugoslavia until the end of the war and on 19 October 1945, No.5 Squadron was disbanded. No.5 Squadron was not included in the 'modern' battle order.

No.5 Squadron WW II equipment: *Curtiss Tomahawk IIB, Feb 42 - Jan 43; Curtiss Kittyhawk III, Jan 43 - Dec 43; Kittyhawk IV, Dec 43 - Sep 44. North American Mustang III, Sep 44 - Oct 45; Mustang IV, Mar 45 - Oct 45.*

No. 5 Squadron was the sole operator of the interim Atlas Cheetah E model *(ad astra)*.

12

No.7 Squadron was formed on 12 January 1942, at Zwartkop as a fighter unit with Curtiss Mohawks and left for Egypt in April that year. On 5 May it arrived at Amriya and began to receive Hawker Hurricane Is, operations beginning on 4 July. After a period in the Western Desert, in September 1942, the squadron began working up with Hurricane IID tank-busters equipped with 40 mm cannon, although in November most of these were being replaced by Mk IIC night fighters, many of which had only two wing-mounted cannon fitted to reduce weight, in an attempt to improve performance.

As the Eighth Army moved through Libya, No.7 Squadron followed providing fighter cover and protection for coastal re-supply convoys. In April 1943, tank-busting Mk IIDs again formed the basis of the squadrons inventory but the Axis forces in North Africa surrendered before any operations could be mounted. The squadrons equipment subsequently reverted to Hurricane Mk IICs. In July 1943, these were supplanted with Supermarine Spitfire VCs with the squadron now based in Palestine and in September it sent a detachment to Kos in the Aegean where small enemy forces had landed to occupy the island. Unfortunately in a German counter-attack the complete detachment was lost. Nevertheless, in November a further detachment moved to Cyprus and took part in fighter sweeps over the island of Rhodes while other Spitfires provided air cover for the Cairo Conference. In April 1944, the squadron moved to Italy where it flew escort and ground-attack missions for the remainder of the war.

On the 12 July 1945, No.7 Squadron's personnel joined many of their comrades for shipment back to South Africa. Japans surrender in August 1945, led to disbandment of the unit on 10 September 1945 preventing a planned attachment to Commonwealth Forces in Ceylon (Sri Lanka) in preparation for the invasion of Malaya. No.7 Squadron was not included in the 'modern' battle order.

No.7 Squadron WW II equipment: *Hawker Hurricane I, May 42 - Dec 4; Hurricane IIB, Jul 42 - Sep 42; Hurricane IID, Sep 42 - Jan 43, Apr 43 - May 43. Hawker Hurricane IIC Dec 42 - Aug 43; Supermarine Spitfire VC, Jul 43 - Mar 44; Spitfire IX, Nov 43 - Dec 43, Mar 44 - Jul 45.*

No.9 Squadron was formed at Almaza, Egypt on 19 May 1944, and moved almost immediately to Syria to receive its Supermarine Spitfires in June and the squadron returned to Egypt by the end of the month. It was immediately deployed on air defence duties in the Eastern Mediterranean in addition to guarding the Egyptian coast and the Suez Canal. It also sent detachments to Cyprus and Palestine. A number of Spitfire IXs were added to the squadron's inventory at this time to combat high-altitude enemy reconnaissance planes. In December 1944, the squadron took part in fighter sweeps over the Greek island of Crete but was disbanded on 1 February, 1945. No.9 Squadron was not included in the 'modern' battle order. No. 9 Squadron WW II equipment: *Supermarine Spitfire VB, VC, Jun 44 - Feb 45; Spitfire IX, Jul 44 - Feb 45.*

Supermarine Spitfires were used extensively by the SAAF fighter squadrons in WWII.

F/sgt PB Vermaak   All-silver Atlas Impala I dual-seat trainer *(ad astra)*

F/sgt PB Vermaak   Camouflaged Atlas Impala II single-seat attack plane *(ad astra)*

14

No.10 Squadron was also formed at Almaza, Egypt on 25 May 1944, as a fighter unit equipped with Supermarine Spitfires. It received operational training in Syria in June and moved back to Egypt at the end of the month to fly air defence and convoy patrols. A number of Mk IX Spitfires were taken on inventory for high-altitude interception duties in July and in September 1944, the squadron moved to Libya. In October 1944, it flew armed reconnaissance sweeps over Crete but on 31st of the month the unit handed its airplanes over to No. 9 Squadron and its personnel were dispersed to other units. No.10 Squadron was not included in the 'modern' battle order.

No.10 Squadron WW II equipment: *Supermarine Spitfire VB, VC, Jun 44 - Oct 44; Spitfire IX, Jul 44 - Oct 44.*

No.11 Squadron was formed on 11 December 1939, at Waterkloof as an army co-operation unit with locally-built armoured Hawker Hartbees biplanes and moved to Kenya in May 1940, to serve alongside the RAF for defence against the Italian colonial forces being strengthened in East Africa. On 11 June 1940, the day following Italy's entry into the War, twenty-five SAAF Hartbees (from Nos 11 and 12 Light Bomber Squadrons) flew pre-emptive bombing raids against the Italians at Royale on the Kenyan border with Ethiopia, and on Banda Hill nearby. Later in June 1940, the squadron converted to Fairey Battle monoplane bombers and took part in the South African campaign in Italian Somaliland and Ethiopia until May 1941, when it was re-numbered No.15 Squadron.

A new No.11 Squadron reformed on 29 June 1944, at Almaza, Egypt, as a fighter squadron equipped with Supermarine Spitfires. Later, on 1 September 1944, the ground echelon left for Italy where it joined the Desert Air Force, the air element re-equipping with Curtiss Kittyhawks in October. Operations began on 30th October with the squadron forming part of No. 8 (SAAF) Wing. For the rest of the war the squadron was engaged in close support missions with the Allied armies and flew fighter-bomber sweeps on strategic targets over northern Italy.

In August 1945, the squadron converted to Spitfire IXs which were flown to Egypt in September 1945, to link up with the units ground echelon, but following the Japanese surrender, on 30 October 1945, the squadron disbanded. No.11 Squadron was not included in the 'modern' battle order.

No.11 Squadron WW II equipment: *Supermarine Spitfire VB, VC, Jul 44 - Aug 44; Curtiss Kittyhawk IV, Oct 44 - Aug 45; Supermarine Spitfire IX, Aug 45 - Oct 45.*

No.12 Squadron was first formed in December 1939 at Waterkloof, and equipped with armoured Hartbees was co-located north to Kenya in 1940, with No.11 Squadron for operations against the Italians. Later in the year it was at Waterkloof with Avro Ansons for coastal reconnaissance, until re-equipped with requisitioned South African Airways Junkers Ju-86, before leaving for Kenya again as a heavy bomber unit. As the campaign in East Africa drew to a close the squadron converted to American Martin A-22 Marylands and moved to the Middle East.

On the 28 May 1941, it arrived at Shandur and later moved to the first of a number of advanced landing grounds in the Western Desert that it would operate from for more than a year to attack enemy positions and bases behind the lines. Early in 1942, it converted to Douglas Bostons and was continuously engaged in bombing operations from the 15 March, until the end of the North African campaign. Following the Axis surrender in Tunisia, the squadron moved to Malta to support the Allied landings in Sicily and Italy. In October it moved into captured Italian bases to continue its day and night attacks against enemy targets.

In January 1944, No.12 converted to Martin Marauder medium-bombers to undertake a series of daylight raids as part of No.3 (SAAF) Wing against road and rail centres, ports and industrial targets. At the wars end in 1945, the squadron began to ferry its airplanes back to Egypt, where the last airplane arrived on 5 November 1945, as the units personnel moved back to South Africa. No.12 Squadron was not included in the 'modern' battle order. No.12 Squadron WW II equipment:

Martin Maryland II, May 41 - Mar 42; Douglas Boston III, Mar 42 - Dec 43. Martin Marauder II, Jun 44 - Dec 44; Martin Marauder III, Aug 44 - Nov 45. Note: British Air Ministry wartime unit Identification Code 'VL' was carried for a period.

No.15 Squadron arrived in Egypt on 13 February 1942 from East Africa where it had flown "modern" Fairy Battles during the operations in Italian Somaliland and Ethiopia. After conversion to Marylands to become a tactical bomber unit it joined the Desert Air Force re-equipping with Bristol Blenheim IVs and kept a continuous detachment deep in the desert at Kufra Oasis to protect the southern flank of the Eighth Army. In July it re-equipped with Bristol Blenheim Vs to fly ASW patrols off the Egyptian coast.

In May 1943, Martin Baltimores supplanted the Blenheims and on 27 August the squadron started shipping strikes over the Aegean Sea. However, anti-submarine patrols were also maintained until the 14 July, 1944.

With the decline of enemy shipping in the region No.15 Squadron moved to Italy to become a day bomber squadron flying its first mission on 20 August, 1944. Attacks on enemy rail and road links were undertaken until February 1945, when the squadron switched to night interdiction missions, as daylight enemy movements had almost ceased, and these missions occupied the squadron until the wars end.

On the 16 July 1945, the squadron was stood down and its airplanes were flown out. Two weeks later its personnel embarked on their passage to South Africa, to formally disband there, on 9 August 1945.

In 2003, No.15 Squadron formed part of the SAAF's 'modern' battle order equipped with Atlas Oryx and Eurocopter (MBB) BK 117 helicopters, at Durban AFB

No.15 Squadron WW II equipment: *Fairey Battle 1941/42; Bristol Blenheim IV, Feb 42 - Apr 43; Blenheim V, Jul 42 - Jul 43.*
Martin Baltimore IIIA, IV, V, May 43 - Jul 45. Note: British Air Ministry wartime unit Identification Code 'ZP' was carried for a period.

No. 15 Squadron operates the Atlas Oryx 'Super Puma' in the modern battle order. *(T. Shia).*

No.16 Squadron was first formed at Germiston on 14 September 1939, as a coastal reconnaissance unit equipped with some of the Junkers Ju 86s requisitioned from South African Airways. In December 1939, it was absorbed into No.32 Squadron. It reformed on 1 May 1941, at Addis Ababa with Ju 86s and Maryland light bombers relinquished by No.12 Squadron. However, as Italian resistance in East Africa diminished, the unit disbanded on 22 August 1941. On the 4 September the following year No.20 Squadron in Madagascar was re-numbered No.16 Squadron. Equipped with Bristol Beauforts and Martin Marylands, it provided close air support for the army during the occupation of the island.

In November 1942, it moved to Kilifi in Kenya, the first three airplanes arriving on the 8 November. Conversion to Bristol Blenheim Vs began and coastal patrols were flown before relocation to Egypt began on 14 April, 1945. The ground echelon left on 20 April and arrived at Landing Ground 91 (L.G.91) on 7 May, to join the air element which had flown up through the Sudan.

The Bristol Beauforts received in June 1943, were deployed on ASW duties and were not used as torpedo-bombers but were flown on anti-shipping patrols until December 1943, when rocket-firing Bristol Beaufighters began to equip the squadron. The Beaufighters were deployed on anti-shipping sweeps over the Aegean Sea in February 1944. As the enemy shipping movements in the area declined the squadron moved to Italy for operations over the Adriatic as part of the Balkan Air Force. In addition to shipping No.16 Squadron also gave support to Yugoslav partisans by attacking German encampments and their communication centres. At the wars end the squadron disbanded on 15 June, 1945. In 2003, No.16 Squadron formed part of the SAAF's 'modern' battle order equipped with Atlas Rooivalk CSH-2 attack helicopters at Bloemspruit AFB.

No 16 Squadron WW II equipment: *Bristol Blenheim V, Nov 42 - Jun 43; Bristol Beaufort I , Jun 43 - Nov 43; Bristol Beaufighter X, Dec 43 - Jun 45.*

No. 16 Squadron are the sole operators of the Atlas Rooivalk attack helicopter *(author)*

No.17 Squadron first formed on 1 September 1939, at Zwartkop to fly Junkers Ju 52/3m transport planes acquired from South African Airways. Two months later the unit merged with Nos.18 and 19 Squadrons to form No.50 Squadron.

No.17 Squadron reformed at Zwartkop on 8 October 1942, immediately embarking for Aden to equip with Bristol Blenheim Vs for anti-submarine patrols. In May 1943, these airplanes were flown to Egypt where they were subsequently replaced by Lockheed Venturas. Until the Venturas arrived for a short period SAAF aircrews were attached to Allied transport units but with the arrival of Venturas in August anti-submarine patrols began, with the airplanes based in Palestine. In April 1944, the squadron moved to the Western Mediterranean and was based at Gibraltar where its airplanes deployed to carry out ASW patrols along the north Italian coast and the French Riveria. Later, based in Sardinia and Italy for bombing coastal targets it also undertook escort duties and air-sea-rescue patrols.

January 1945, saw a major redeployment of the squadron with the ground echelon moved to Algiers while the Venturas flew to Egypt becoming non-operational on 23 February. The ground echelon now transferred to Gianaclis in April 1945, to receive RAF ASR Warwicks, but initially some Vickers Wellingtons were supplied until Warwicks became available. Conversion on type commenced in May but the war in Europe had ended and the squadron prepared to leave for South Africa on 2 September, 1945. On arrival at Ysterplaat, Cape Province, it disbanded on 31 March 1946, control of the equipment having been handed over to the SAAF on 7 October, 1945. In 2003, No.17 Squadron formed part of the SAAF's 'modern' battle order equipped with Alouette III, Atlas Oryx helicopters and a single SA 365N Dauphin helicopter.

No.17 Squadron WW II equipment: *Bristol Blenheim V, Jun 43 - May 43;Lockheed Ventura V, Aug 43 - Feb 45.*
Vickers Wellington XII, May 45 - Sep 45; Vickers Warwick V, May 45 - Mar 46.

F/sgt PB Vermaak   No. 17 Squadron Alouette III are now (2002/3) mainly used for rescue duties *(ad astra).*

No.19 Squadron was formed on 12 August 1944, by renumbering No. 227 Squadron RAF at Biferno, Italy. During the previous weeks SAAF personnel gradually replaced RAF personnel in the squadron. Equipped with Bristol Beaufighters, the squadron was used to attack enemy targets in Yugoslavia, Albania and northern Greece in support of partisan forces.

In February 1945, as part of the Balkan Air Force, under the command of Lt-Col Don Tilley DFC the squadron was called on to devise a plan to sink the 4,200 ton SS *Kuckuck,* a Nazi ship that was being fitted with large guns in the Yugoslavian port of Fiume. It was known from reports that had come through from Yugoslavian Partisan Forces that Fiume was heavily defended. They reported that around 150 anti-aircraft guns were defending the port area - 20mm, 40mm and 88mm guns were strategically placed specifically to deal with Allied air attacks. Having devised his plan, Tilley, selected three of his most experienced pilots for the mission, men who had proved themselves to be cool-headed under attack and capable of hitting small targets. Major Geater, Captain Dickson and Captain Steve Stevens. Normally eight Beaufighters would have been assigned to deal with such an important target, but Don Tilley knew that if there were more than four airplanes involved, there would be little chance of the others getting back without being holed or shot down.

Flying in overland at low level to avoid detection by the German radar, it felt to the crews as if every anti-aircraft gun possible was firing at them. Nevertheless, Lt-Col Tilley who had already sunk a considerable tonnage of enemy shipping including at least one oil tanker, fired his salvo of eight 3-in rocket projectiles holing the *Kuckuck* below the water line. On recovery to base, photographs from the Beaufighters nose cameras revealed the success of the mission, confirmed the next morning by a high-flying reconnaissance RAF Spitfire. A few days later Lt-Col Tilley was awarded the DSO.

The squadron continued its attacks on enemy shipping along the Adriatic coast as well as land communications targets throughout 1945, until the wars end. Unfortunately shortly after the sinking of the *Kuckuck,* Captain Dickson, was killed when the squadron was attacking Cernik Castle at the time of a conference by twelve Nazi generals.

In March 1945, the Yugoslav Partisans heard that the Nazis were planning to hold a battle strategy conference involving twelve top Generals, and Cernik Castle had been selected as the venue. The Partisans sent a message to the Balkan Air Force headquarters asking for an attack on this Castle in the hope that some of the gathered Nazis 'top brass', would be killed. No.19 Squadron SAAF was chosen to carry out the attack, their suitability to undertake such a high profile mission already well established with the raid on the SS *Kuckuck.*

A few days later No.19 Squadron received a message from the Partisans to say that Nazis staff cars had been seen to converge on Cernik Castle. It was time to launch the attack. After a final briefing of the eight Beaufighter pilots and their navigators - who also acted as wireless operators and air gunners - the crews were taken to the dispersals where the airplanes had been readied for the mission. Once airborne the Beaufighters headed out over the the Adriatic for Yugoslavia, hoping the unusually good weather in the area would hold. As the squadron approached the target they dropped down to tree-top level to avoid detection by enemy radar. As the castle and surrounding area was not very heavily guarded by anti-aircraft guns, the squadron did not consider it to be a very dangerous target to attack. But, they also suspected that special big guns would have been brought in for such a conference of high-ranking Nazi officers, so the airplanes closed in not only to surprise those gathered but also to get through and execute a concerted attack so quickly they would not have time to bring the guns to bear on the Beaufighters.

The leading Beaufighter was piloted by Lt Col Don Tilley who was one of the most experienced and the most highly decorated pilots in the Balkan Air Force. Having just received his DSO for his part in the sinking of the SS *KuckucK*. Flying in fast with their propellers almost clipping the tree-tops, suddenly Cernik Castle appeared right in front of them. When they were within half a mile of it, Lt Col Tilley pulled his Bristol Beaufighter up almost vertically increasing altitude by around two hundred feet, with the others in pursuit. This was deemed the best way to attack the castle and the following airplanes could see the leaders rocket salvos ripping into the castle roof. Suddenly radio silence was broken with someone shouting out, "Dickies been shot down". Captain Dickson who had survived the 'suicide' attack on the SS *Kuckuck*, when the air was thick with anti-aircraft fire, was down. Again, No.19 Squadron had carried out a text book attack, but one of the team had been brought down. Almost instinctively one of the Beaufighters piloted by Steve Schonveldt at great risk to himself, his navigator and his Beaufighter, returned to the scene after his attack to take low-level pictures of the downed Beaufighter.

Meeting up back at their base at Biferno, on the Italian coast at Termoli, Schonveldt reported, as was apparent from the photographs he had took, there was little hope that Captain Dickson or his RAF navigator, Flying Officer Brace, survived the crash. On notification that further photographs from the Beaufighters excellent nose cameras had been developed, it was obvious to all that both airmen must have been killed in the crash.

The next day, the Yugoslav Partisans reported that they had watched the Beaufighters fly in on their attack and on seeing Captain Dickson's plane go in, had jumped in their American-supplied jeep and raced down to the scene of the crash, hoping to get there before the Germans. When they arrived they were amazed to see F/O Brace standing beside the wrecked airplane with only a black-eye. The only recognisable part of the fighter-bomber still intact, was a section of the fuselage ! Captain Dickson, unfortunately was not so lucky, being found still strapped into his seat. Having recovered his body and with F/O Brace aboard they left the scene as quickly as possible. Within a few days Brace was on his way to Allied-held territory in northern Italy and he was flown back to the UK.

At the same time the squadron received a grateful message from the Partisans that the attack had been successful and at least three of the twelve Nazi Generals had been killed. Fortunately as the German fighting machine in the Balkans at this time was on the verge of collapse, there were no reprisals. The Germans in all probability hoping they themselves would be treated with similar 'mercy', if captured. With the war over, on the 10 July 1945, the squadron was disbanded and its personnel returned to South Africa. In 2003, No.19 Squadron formed part of the SAAF's 'modern' battle order equipped with Alouette III and Atlas Oryx helicopters at Louis Trichardt AFB.

No.19 Squadron WW II equipment: *Bristol Beaufighter X, XI, Aug 44 - Jul 45.*

SAAF Aerospatiale Alouette IIIs were used devoid of all markings in the Rhodesian Border Wars. (ad astra)

No.21 Squadron was formed at Nakuru on 8 May 1941, as a light bomber unit equipped with Martin Maryland IIs. During July, its airplanes and ground echelons moved to Egypt and assembled at Shandur. After familiarisation training in desert conditions, the unit flew its first operational sortie on 24 September 1941. Attacks on enemy bases and airfields continued until January 1942, when the unit was withdrawn to re-equip with Martin Baltimores.

The Baltimores failed to materialise and the squadrons ground crews were used for repair and maintenance work on airplanes at other units. However, for a few weeks in March and April, some Baltimores were loaned to the squadron but it was not until August that any prolonged serious flying could be undertaken. Nevertheless, on 20 October 1942, No. 21 Squadron flew its first operational Baltimore mission and these continued for the rest of the campaign in North Africa, the airplanes striking at enemy communications, and battlefield positions, bases and supply depots behind the front. Some night interdiction missions were also flown, in early 1943. In July 1943, the squadron moved to Malta to support the Allied invasion of Sicily but the ground echelon remained in North Africa until it moved to Sicily to join with the air element. Later the squadron moved into captured Italian airfields to continue tactical day bombing operations. In July 1944, the Baltimores were replaced with Martin Marauders which flew their first operational mission on 15 August, 1944. For the rest of the war the squadron operated the type to attack road and rail communication targets in northern Italy.

Following VE Day No. 21 Squadron was engaged in flying on communications duties before officially disbanding on 10 September, 1945. Despite this the squadron continued to fly and moved to Egypt between 22 and 30 September, where its personnel finally embarked for South Africa. In 2003, No.21(VIP) Squadron formed part of the SAAF's 'modern' battle order equipped with two Dassault Falcon 50s, an long-range Boeing Biz Jet and two Cessna 550 Citation IIs.

No. 21 Squadron WW II equipment: *Martin Maryland II, May 41 - Feb 42; Martin Baltimore III, IV, Aug 42 - Jul 44; Martin Marauder II, III, Jul 44 - Sep 45.*

Latest addition to No. 21 (VIP) Squadrons inventory is the Boeing Biz Jet.

No.22 Squadron was formed on 1 July 1942 at Durban for general reconnaissance duties with Avro Ansons and Junkers Ju 86s but soon re-equipped with Lockheed Venturas. In June 1944, the squadron was transferred to Gibraltar and began flying ASW patrols. These were maintained until the end of the war and in July 1945, No.22 Squadron moved to Egypt where it disbanded on 24 October, 1945. In 2003, No.22 Squadron formed part of the SAAF's 'modern' battle order equipped with Alouette III, Atlas Oryx and two SA 330J Puma helicopters at Ysterplaat AFB.

No. 22 Squadron WW II equipment: *Lockheed Ventura V, Jun 44 - Oct 45.*

No.24 Squadron was formed at Nakuru, Kenya, on 5 March 1941, its air element moving to Egypt to equip with Martin Marylands on 19 March 1941. The ground echelon left South Africa on 16 May by which time No.24 Squadron's airplanes had begun to operate in the Western Desert attached to No.39 Squadron RAF. Tactical bombing by day and occasional night operations were flown until November when the unit converted to Bostons. Throughout its time in North Africa No.24 Squadron operated in support of the Eighth Army bombing enemy positions, airfields, bases and supply dumps in the area.

In July 1943, the squadron moved to Malta for operations over Sicily, having arrived in August to support the Allied landings in Italy. Later moving into captured airfields in Italy it continued operations until flying its last operational mission with Bostons on 8 November. Conversion to Martin Marauders began in December and these were used to attack rail and road targets until the end of the war, the squadron flying its last bombing raid on 25 April, 1945.

On conversion for transport duties its Marauders flew on communication duties in theatre until it moved back to Egypt in October 1945, where the squadron finally disbanded on 6 November that year. No.24 Squadron was not included in the 'modern' battle order. No. 24 Squadron WW II equipment: *Martin Maryland II, Mar 41 - Nov 41; Douglas Boston III, Nov 41 - Dec 43; Martin Marauder II, III, Dec 43 - Nov 45.*

Note: British Air Ministry wartime unit Identification Code 'OZ' was carried for a period.

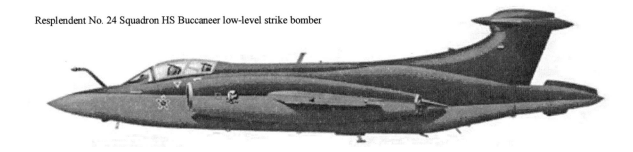

Resplendent No. 24 Squadron HS Buccaneer low-level strike bomber

For maritime strike the squadrons Buccaneers were equipped with Nord AS.30 air-to-surface missiles

No.25 Squadron formed on 1 July 1942, at Port Elizabeth from No.33 Flight for coastal reconnaissance duties. On 12 May 1944, the squadron personnel embarked for the Mediterranean and arrived in Naples on 9 June. In the meantime its Lockheed Venturas flew up from the Union, all nineteen having arrived at Pomigliano by the 9 July. Although intended to operate as an ASW unit, the decrease in enemy activity in the area resulted in no patrols being flown. Instead, the ASW equipment was removed from the airplanes and on 30 August based at Biferno the squadron transferred to the Balkan Air Force to undertake bombing operations over Yugoslavia until the wars end. The squadron returned to South Africa and disbandment on 15 July, 1945. No.25 Squadron was not included in the 'modern' battle order. No. 25 Squadron WW II equipment: *Lockheed Ventura I, Jul 44 - Dec 44; Martin Marauder III, Oct 44 - Jul 45.*

No.26 Squadron was formed on 24 August 1942, at Voortrekkerhoogte as a bomber-reconnaissance unit and embarked for West Africa on 9 April 1943, arriving at Takoradi on 4 May 1943. Equipped with Vickers Wellington XI it flew its first operational patrol on 29 May and for the rest of the war was engaged in ASW patrols off the West African coast. Throughout its operational career in the area the squadron operated from a number of airfields between Dakar and Lagos, but its home base remained at Takoradi.

On 26 May 1945, No.26 Squadron ceased operations and its personnel embarked for South Africa on 30 May, its airplanes being flown to the Middle East for disposal. No.26 Squadron was not included in the 'modern' battle order. No.26 Squadron WW II equipment: *Vicker Wellington XI, May 43 - May 45.*

No.27 Squadron was formed on 24 August 1942, at Eerste River, Cape Province, as a coastal reconnaissance unit equipped with Lockheed Venturas. On 13 June 1944, its ground echelon arrived at La Senia, Algeria, to reinforce the ASW operations in the Western Mediterranean, followed on 6 July by its airplanes. On 11 July it handed over its ageing Ventura IVs to No. 162 Maintenance Unit to take over the newer Mk V variants of No.500 (County of Kent) Squadron RAF.

Operations began on 18 July to fly ASW and ASR missions and on 16 August a large detachment was sent to Malta for two months. On 24 and 25 November 1944, twenty airplanes flew to Egypt and in January 1945, they continued on their way back to South Africa. The ground echelon arrived at Almaza on 24 January and later moved to Gianaclis to prepare for re-equipment with Warwicks. Instead, eight Vickers Wellingtons were supplied in lieu of Warwicks the first airplane arriving on 11 March. Conversion to ASR Warwicks finally began in July for the unit to undertake air-sea-rescue duties in the Eastern Mediterranean. In November 1945, this task was taken over by No. 621 Squadron RAF and No.27 Squadron flew its sixteen Vickers Warwicks back to South Africa where it disbanded in December, 1945. No.27 Squadron was not included in the 'modern' battle order.

No. 27 Squadron WW II equipment: *Lockheed Ventura IV, Aug 42 - Jul 44; Ventura V, Jul 44 - Jan 45;Vickers Wellington XIV, Feb 45 - Mar 45; Vickers Warwick Mar 45 - Dec 45.*

Piaggio P166S Albatross were operated on inland coastal patrol duties by No. 27 Squadron until disbandment

No.28 Squadron was formed at Alamza on 1 June 1943, as a transport unit, from personnel provided by Nos.34 and 35 Flights SAAF. At the end of the month it moved to Castel Benito and by the end of July it had a mixed inventory of Avro Ansons, Vickers Wellingtons and Douglas Dakotas. During August it completed its full complement of twenty Ansons, which were used for communication duties in North Africa, while the Wellingtons and Dakotas were used on long-range flights. However, by the end of the year the rather elderly Wellingtons were withdrawn from use. More C-47 Dakotas were received and by April 1944 the squadron was fully equipped with Dakota transports, with the last of the Ansons departed, although these did return for nine months in January 1945, converted for use as air ambulances.

In June 1944, the squadron moved to Algiers and in the following months it withdrew all its detached airplanes back to base at Maison Blanche, from where it operated a total of thirty Dakota transports on passenger and freight services throughout the Mediterranean area. These services continued after the end of the war and in September 1945, the airplanes and some ground crews returned to South Africa while its remaining personnel returned by sea. Control of the airplanes passing from No.216 Group Communications Flight (RAF), to the SAAF on 30 September 1945. In 2003, No.28 Squadron formed part of the SAAF's 'modern' battle order equipped with Lockheed C-130 Hercules transports at Waterkloof AFB.

No. 28 Squadron WW II equipment: *Vickers Wellington IC, Jul 43 - Dec 43; Avro Anson I, Jul 43 - Apr 44, Jan 45 - Aug 45.*
Douglas Dakota I, II, III, Jul 43 - Sep 45. Beech Expediter I, Feb 45 - May 45.

No.30 Squadron was formed at Pescara on 12 August 1944, as a medium bomber unit equipped with Martin Marauders. It began operations on 25 August and for the rest of the war took part in all aspects of the Italian campaign, except for a break from operational flying between 15 October and 22 November, 1944. On 15 July 1945, No.30 Squadron disbanded. It was not included in the 'modern' battle order. No. 30 Squadron WW II equipment: *Martin Marauder III, Aug 44 - Jul 45.*

No.31 Squadron formed in South Africa during January 1944, and arrived in Egypt on 19 February, for operation as a heavy bomber unit. While its aircrew underwent operational training in Palestine, its American Consolidated Liberator bombers began to arrive. Operations over Crete and the Aegean began on 27 May, but in June the squadron moved to Italy, from where it operated for the rest of the war. It was mainly engaged in bombing raids, mainly at night, on targets in Romania, Austria, Yugoslavia and northern Italy. Supply-dropping missions were also carried out in support of partisan forces in Yugoslavia and northern Italy, as well as mining of the River Danube.

With No.34 Squadron and other RAF and Polish units, No.31 took part in the airlift of supplies to the besieged Polish Home Army in Warsaw in August and September, 1944. Extremely heavy enemy anti-aircraft fire resulted in many airplanes lost over the city and to night fighter activity, while en-route to the dropping zones.

At the end of the war the squadron redeployed on to transport duties to transport British PoWs to the UK and South African troops via Egypt back to the Union. On 8 September 1945, its airplanes began moving squadron personnel to Shallufa, the transfer completed by the end of the month. After a further period of transport duties, in the Mediterranean theatre, the squadron disbanded on 15 December 1945. No.31 Squadron was not included in the 'modern' battle order.

No. 31 Squadron WW II equipment: *Consolidated Liberator VI, Apr 44 - Dec 45.*

SAAF WWII Supermarine Spitfire Mk VC 'WR' of No. 40 Squadron.

Note fuselage mounted recce-camera

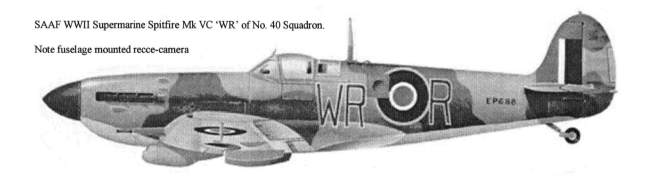

No.34 Squadron was formed at Almaza on 14 April 1944, from personnel arriving from South Africa for heavy bomber operations. Its first Consolidated Liberators arrived in June and at the beginning of July the airplanes flew to Italy to link up with No.31 Squadron to form No.2 (SAAF) Wing at Celone. Its first operation was flown on 21 July even though the ground echelon did not arrive until 26 July. Mainly night bombing missions were flown for the rest of the war over Czechoslovakia, Hungary, northern Italy and Austria. Mine-laying of the Danube and supply-dropping in support of the partisan forces in Yugoslavia and northern Italy were also undertaken. The squadron also operated in concert with No.31 Squadron and other Allied units to fly supplies to the Polish forces besieged in Warsaw in August and September, 1944.

As soon as the war ended the bombers were redeployed to fly supplies to the army in northern Italy and Austria, as well as repatriation flights of freed POWs to Britain and the transfer of South African troops back home via Egypt. In company with its sister squadron the entire wing moved back to Egypt during September 1945, and after undertaking further transport duties in theatre, the squadron and wing disbanded on 15 December, 1945. No.34 Squadron was not included in the 'modern' battle order.

No. 34 Squadron WW II equipment: *Consolidated Liberator VI, Apr 44 - Dec 45.*

No. 34 Squadron Consolidated Liberator B.VI long-range heavy bomber

No.40 Squadron was first formed on 30 May 1940, at Waterkloof as an army co-operation unit with armoured Hartbees. Almost immediately the squadron moved north to Kenya and took part in operations against Italian Somaliland and Ethiopia before returning to the Union in August 1941.

Reformed as a fighter squadron it moved to Egypt in December 1941, to equip with Hawker Hurricane Is in January 1942, at Burg-el-Arab, supplemented later by a few Curtiss Tomahawk IIB. In August 1942, the squadron was withdrawn to re-equip with Hawker Hurricane IIBs before resuming operations. After the Allied breakthrough at El Alamein the squadron was heavily engaged in flying low-level reconnaissance sweeps in order to locate retreating enemy units, and No.40 remained with the Eighth Army until the North African campaign ended.

By February 1943, the squadron had received some Supermarine Spitfire V fighters and by the time it moved to Malta in June, it was fully equipped with this type to fly tactical reconnaissance missions in support of the Allied landings in Sicily in July. It also flew some offensive sweeps and after a short stay on the island it moved to Italy in September 1943, to fly ground-attack and tactical reconnaissance missions in support of the Eighth Army again. In December 1944, the squadron sent a detachment to Greece to support the Allied forces which had re-occupied the mainland.

Following the German surrender in Italy, the squadron flew reconnaissance missions along the Yugoslav border until it disbanded on 20 October 1945, passing its airplanes to No.225 Squadron RAF for use on occupation duties. No.40 Squadron was not included in the 'modern' battle order.

No. 40 Squadron WW II equipment: *Hartbees 1940/41; Hawker Hurricane I, Jan 42 - Aug 42; Curtiss Tomahawk IIB,*
Mar 42 - Aug 42; Supermarine Spitfire VB, VC, Feb 43 - Jun 43; Spitfire IX, Jun 43 - Oct 45; Supermarine Spitfire XI,
Sep 45 - Oct 45. Note: British Air Ministry wartime unit Identification Code 'WR' was carried for a period.

No.41 Squadron was formed on 16 October 1940, at Waterkloof for service in East Africa as an army co-operation unit. Equipped with locally-built armoured Hartbees, it remained in the area until after the Italian surrender, receiving some Curtiss Mohawks before converting to Hawker Hurricane Is.

Meanwhile, on 20 April 1943, the squadron's ground crew left from Port Reitz, Kenya, for Egypt, arriving on 6 May. At the same time its air echelon flew up to Egypt through Sudan where their Mk I Hurricanes were replaced by Mk IIBs for air defence duties. Apart from a single sweep over Crete flown on 23 July the squadron remained on air defence tasks until 1944, when in February, a number of Supermarine Spitfire IXs were received for high-altitude interception duties.

In April 1944, it converted fully to Spitfires and detachments were provided to Palestine and Cyprus. In August 1944, the entire squadron moved to Palestine but between 5 and 8 November batches of personnel left for the SAAF depot at Almaza. The squadron subsequently disbanding at the end of the month. In 2003, No.41 Squadron formed part of the SAAF's 'modern' battle order equipped with Cessna C.208 Caravan I, Beech King Air 200C (2), 300 (1), and a Pilatus PC 12 at Waterkloof AFB

No. 41 Squadron WW II equipment: *Hartbees 1940/41; Curtiss Mohawks, Hawker Hurricane Is. 41/43; Hawker Hurricane IIB, May 43 - Jul 43;Hurricane IIC, Jul 43 - Mar 44; Supermarine Spitfire IX, Feb 44 - Jul 44. Supermarine Spitfire VC Mar 44 - Nov 44.*

Latest equipment to join No. 41 Squadron is a single Swiss Pilatus PC 12 regional turboprop

No. 44 Squadron was formed on 12 March 1944, from the personnel of No.43 Squadron which had left the Union on the 8 February for Egypt arriving on the 26 February. The ground crew at Almaza received familiarisation training on Douglas Dakota transports. Aircrew were attached to No.28 Squadron for operational training on type. The squadron did not receive its own Dakotas until the 27 April and transport operations finally began on 14 July. This involved the squadron's airplanes operating throughout the Mediterranean, south to the Sudan and East Africa and even to the Soviet Union. At the same time various detachments were sent to Aden, Italy, the Sudan and Iraq.

In December 1944, the detachment at Bari, Italy, began flying supply drops and casualty evacuation missions in support of the Yugoslav partisans. Between 1 and 11 February 1945, the squadron relocated all its airplanes and personnel to Italy as a complete unit and remained there until the end of the war. At this time a few Avro Ansons were received for communications and air ambulance duties. After the German surrender the squadron continued operations until 7 December 1945, when the first airplanes left for Cairo. Next day, the units task was taken over by the RAF and No.44 Squadron's airplanes continued to return to Egypt en-route for the Union, the last leaving Bari on 11 December, 1945.

In 2003, No.44 Squadron formed part of the SAAF's 'modern' battle order equipped with Casa C.212 Aviocar, Casa CN 235 (1), and C-160 Transall (4) at Waterkloof AFB.

No. 44 Squadron WW II equipment: *Douglas Dakota III, Apr 44 - Dec 45; Avro Anson XII, Mar 45 - Aug 45.*

No.60 Squadron assembled at Heliopolis, Egypt, in July 1941 as a reconnaissance unit equipped with Martin Marylands, having previously been deployed as a photographic survey unit in East Africa with Avro Ansons. In addition to photographic reconnaissance work in the Western Desert the squadron undertook survey flights over friendly territory and in January 1942, it was withdrawn from front-line duties to concentrate entirely on its survey tasks. Eventually most of its airplanes were withdrawn and at one time the squadron was virtually grounded. However, in October 1942, some Martin Baltimores were received and these were used to map enemy defensive positions, including large sections of the Mareth line, as the Eighth Army continued its advance through Libya to Tunisia. In February 1943, the Baltimores were supplemented with D.H. Mosquitoes to afford the crews a degree of self protection whilst flying over hostile territory by way of the de Havilland airplanes better turn of speed. By the mid-summer of 1943, the squadron had fully re-equipped with Mosquitoes and by the time Italy was invaded the squadron was carrying out photographic reconnaissance missions over France, Italy and Yugoslavia.

In December 1943, the squadron moved to San Severo, Italy from where it flew long-range photographic reconnaissance missions over Italy, Austria and Germany for the rest of the war. On 3 August 1945, control of the squadron passed to the SAAF and on 22 August it airplanes left for the Union of South Africa. In 2003, No.60 Squadron formed part of the SAAF's 'modern' battle order equipped with five Boeing B.707-328s at Waterkloof AFB.

No. 60 Squadron WW II equipment:

Martin Maryland I, II, Aug 41 - Jun 43;Martin Baltimore II, Oct 42 - Jun 43; Martin Baltimore III, Oct 42 - Aug 43.
D.H. Mosquito IV, Feb 43 - Oct 43; D.H. Mosquito VI, Jul 43 - Dec 43; D.H. Mosquito IX, Jul 43 - Sep 44; D.H. Mosquito XVI,
Feb 44 - Aug 45.

No. 60 Squadron B.707-328 force multiplier 'tops up' a No. 2 Squadron Cheetah D airplane *(T. Shia)*

In concluding our brief review of SAAF operations in World War II, mention should be made of two very important South African airmen who flew their war with the RAF. Group Captain Adolph 'Sailor' Malan (1910-64) and Squadron Leader Marmaduke Thomas St. John 'Pat' Pattle (1914-41). Both airmen were WW II 'aces', Malan with an estimated 32 "kills"and Pattle with an estimated 51.

Born in Butterworth, South Africa, Pattle, left for Britain to join the RAF in 1936. After completing his flying training, he joined No.80 Squadron flying Gloster Gladiator biplane fighters and accompanied the squadron to Egypt in the spring of 1938. When Italy entered the war, Pattle was a flight commander. He first saw action on 4 August 1940, shooting down an Italian Fiat CR 32 biplane fighter and a Breda Ba 65 fighter-bomber, but then was forced to bale out of his damaged Gladiator. Having landed behind enemy lines, he evaded capture and made his way back to Allied lines. On the 8 August he was back in the air again and shot down two Fiat CR 42 fighters.

In November 1940, No.80 Squadron was sent to Greece to help repel the Italian invaders. Pattle was in action again on 19 November, claiming two Fiat CR 42s. Further victories followed and by early March 1941, with 23 "kills" to his credit, he was awarded a bar to his DFC and promoted to Squadron Leader. He then assumed command of No.33 Squadron equipped with Hawker Hurricane Is having newly arrived in Greece. Pattle's first mission with the squadron was a bomber escort operation over Albania on 23 March during which he destroyed an Fiat G 50 in the air and a further three during a strafing attack on the airfield. On 6 April 1941, Germany entered the war in the Balkans and the air war in the region increased considerably in intensity. From this time No.33 Squadron were almost continually engaged in aerial combat with Luftwaffe Messerschmitt Bf 109s until it was forced to withdraw from the forward airfields to the Athens area. On 20 April on his third sortie of the day Pattle engaged a formation of German bombers over Eleusis Bay and shot two of them down before his own plane came under attack from a Messerschmitt Bf 110 and he was shot down into the sea.

It is possible Squadron Leader Pattle DFC., was in fact the RAF's leading 'ace', but unfortunately as the records for the period in Greece were lost during the evacuation, official confirmation of Pattle's final tally is impossible. What is certain, is that this little-known South African established himself as an outstanding wartime combat pilot and fittingly his own countrymen have erected a bronze statute in his memory at Durban airport.

On the other hand Group Captain Malan survived the war, and not wishing to remain in the post-war RAF returned to his native South Africa in 1946, to take up farming. He was born at Wellington, South Africa and served as an officer in the Merchant Navy before joining the RAF in 1935. The following year he was commissioned and posted to No.74 (F) Squadron, which flew Gloster Gauntlet biplane fighters from Hornchurch, Essex in the UK. By the outbreak of war in 1939, Malan was a flight commander with the squadron, which was then equipped with Supermarine Spitfires. He first saw action when he covered the evacuation of the British Expeditionary Force from Dunkirk, claiming his first victory on 21 May 1940. On 8 August 1940, he was appointed the squadron's commander and was awarded the DFC for his actions over Dunkirk, later in June 1941 he received a bar to this decoration for shooting down two enemy bombers at night. This was the first time during WW II on which an RAF Fighter Command single-seat day-fighter pilot had scored at night. In July he led No.74 Squadron in the opening skirmishes of the Battle of Britain. The following month the air combats intensified and on the 11 August he shot down two Messerschmitt Bf 109 fighters and two days later a Dornier Do 17 bomber.

Early in 1941, Malan became one of the first wing leaders in Fighter Command and took charge of the famous Biggin Hill squadrons. In June 1941 alone, Malan accounted personally for nine of the enemy Messerschmitt Bf 109 fighters shot down that month. At the end of the summer in 1941, he was taken off operations and awarded a bar to his DSO. At this time he was the highest-scoring fighter pilot in the RAF with 32 "kills". Which remained his official total at the wars end.

He also made a significant contribution to aerial warfare when he drew up and published his *Ten Rules of Air Fighting*, giving valuable guidance on how to win over enemy pilots and, probably more important and uppermost in most fighter pilots minds, how to stay alive!

Flotation gear equipped SA 330 Pumas were alse deployed on (rocky) mountain rescue duties
(ad astra)

2. New Equipment

After the war, the SAAF had a greatly increased inventory comprising ten fighter-bomber squadrons equipped with Supermarine Spitfires, Curtiss Kittyhawks, North American P-51 Mustangs and Bristol Beaufighters, eight bomber squadrons with American Consolidated Liberators, Martin Marauders and Baltimores, one photographic reconnaissance squadron with D.H. Mosquitoes, two transport squadrons with Douglas C-47 Dakotas and three maritime squadrons with Lockheed Venturas and Vickers Wellingtons. At this time three fighter squadrons had already been disbanded to bolster other units and anti-submarine patrols with Short Sunderland and five Ventura squadrons had already been suspended. Many squadrons were disbanded and personnel returned to South Africa, while others transferred to transport duties, returning home with their airplanes that passed out of RAF control. Very quickly the SAAF was reorganised as a small force capable of rapid expansion from the SAAF Reserve and Active Citizen Force personnel. Wartime equipment remained in service for a number of years and the SAAF transport fleet took part in the Berlin Airlift, Operation *Plainfare.*

In 1950, the SAAF sent a small force to fight alongside United Nations forces in Korea, its piston-engined P-51D Mustangs having to face the Soviet-built MiG-15 jets used by the North Koreans. Of the 95 Mustangs purchased by the South African government from the USAF for use in Korea, 73 were lost in combat and 34 of the No.2 Squadrons pilots were listed as either missing in action or killed in action in the conflict. The squadron flew a total of 10,596 sorties in the (P) F-51, making a significant contribution to the UN air efforts during this crucial period of communist aggression. It was in Korea in January 1953, that the SAAF received its first jets, North American F-86F-30 Sabres on loan from the USAF. No.2 Squadrons first F-86 combat sortie was flown on the 22 February 1953, by its commander Ralph Gerneke in company with an 'all star' flight, made up of three USAF squadron commanders and the USAF's 18th Fighter Wing C.O. Colonel Martin. On the final day of the conflict — the 27 July 1953, No.2 Squadron had sixteen F-86 Sabres on inventory and fourteen of them flew 41 combat sorties that day for an outstanding average of 2.93 sorties per airplane. On returning to South Africa later in the year the air arm received de Havilland Vampire FB.5 fighter-bombers with Vampire T.55 jet trainers that started to replace the Supermarine Spitfires still in service. Canadair CL-13B Sabre 6 fighters, de Havilland Dove and Heron transports and Sikorsky S.55 helicopters were delivered in 1956. A notable milestone occurred on the 21 September 1956, when the first CL 13 Sabre jet to take to the skies over South Africa flown by Capt. John Inglesby of No.1 Squadron broke the sound barrier. The following year, the Short Sunderlands were replaced by Avro Shackleton MR.3 maritime-reconnaissance aircraft for defence of the all important Cape shipping routes.

The ubiquitous Short Sunderland flying-boat had entered SAAF service with No.35 Squadron based at Congella, Durban, on the cessation of hostilities in 1945, a number of crews having undergone training on type in the UK. Sixteen Sunderlands were delivered and almost immediately on 26 April 1945, one was damaged beyond repair when it struck the dock in Durban harbour, just one day after its arrival ! By the time of their final retirement in 1957 (most were scrapped in 1955), at least three others were damaged beyond repair. One was lost in the waters of Lake Mzingazi near Richards Bay after attempting a landing at night during a heavy thunderstorm on 1 November 1956, with the loss of two lives.

During the late 1950s, early 1960s, a limited expansion programme was started to maintain a balance of power in Africa where certain newly independent states were displaying hostility towards South Africa. Following a goodwill visit to South Africa by four Avro Shackleton MR.2s of No.204 Squadron RAF in June 1955, and their subsequent evaluation, the SAAF decided the type would be a suitable Short Sunderland replacement. Eight Shackletons were ordered (serials 1716 to 1723) and delivery took place in 1957, to No.35 Squadron now land-based at Ysterplaat, near Cape Town. Flight training was undertaken by forty SAAF personnel in the UK at the A.V. Roe factory at Woodford in 1956, culminating in a period of operational flying with the RAF. On 21 May 1957, at RAF St Mawgan, No.35 Squadron received its first two MR.3s almost three months before the RAF's famous No. 220 Squadron re-equipped with this variant.

The SAAF's first three Shackletons (1716, 1717 and 1718) landed in South Africa on 16 August 1957, at Waterkloof AFB, finally reaching Ysterplaat on the 19th. Two others (serials 1719 and 1720) arrived in October and the last three (1721, 1722 and 1723) on 26 February, 1958. However, problems with airspace congestion and the lack of runway length at Ysterplatt, saw No.35 Squadron relocated to the recently completed D.F. Malan International Airport, Cape Town.

The first border patrol undertaken by a Shackleton set a SAAF non-stop endurance record of 2,900 miles taking 14 hours 30 minutes. The route taken from Waterkloof to Cape Town included Beit Bridge, the Bechuanaland (now Botswana) border, Katima Mulilo (Caprivi Strip) and the South West African (now Namibian) border to the Cuene river mouth. In the 1960s the Avro Shackletons maintained constant surveillance on Soviet naval movements off its coast A well-publicised but ultimately unsuccessful prolonged search for a Russian submarine sighted off the Zululand coast near Richards Bay was undertaken in June 1964, and again in 1965.

For more than a decade throughout the 1970s Shackletons patrolled the South African coast up to the 200 mile fishing limit set in 1971, amounting to a total area of approximately 450,000 square miles. Bearing its pelican emblem and their motto of *Shaya Amanzi* (meaning 'strike the water' in the Zulu language) it was No.35 Squadron's task to patrol South African coastal waters. Many hours were spent on search-and-rescue operations as well as a number of other extraordinary tasks. In 1971, the Liberian tanker *Wafra* with a full load of oil ran onto a shoal at Cape Agulhas. It was pulled off, towed 200 metres out to sea and sunk by a No.35 Squadron Shackleton to minimise pollution of the coastline. After spotting requests for bread written in the sand, Shackleton serial 1720/M dropped food to Angolan refugees stranded on the Skeletan Coast of South West Africa (now Namibia) and on 11 January 1980, Shackletons took part in the rescue of the crew of the grounded Danish ship *Pep Ice* near Bassas da India in the Mozambique Channel.

The squadron was also involved in the world-wide rescue operation set up for the re-entry and splash-down of Apollo 13. At the same time assuming a more passive role, No.35's Shackletons reported on major maritime events in the region such as the Cape to Rio yacht race inaugurated in 1971. In recognition of its service to the community the squadron received the Freedom of the City of Cape Town on 26 June 1980 and was also recommended for another honour, the Sword of Peace on 3 October, 1984. One Shackleton (serial 1718) crashed in the Stettynsberg range of mountains during poor weather conditions on 8 August 1963, during the 'Capex' sea-air exercises, with the loss of all thirteen crew. This was the only Shackleton lost during the types period of service with the SAAF. The surviving seven airplanes remained operational and were constantly upgraded before final retirement on 4 December, 1984. The final SAAF Shackleton flight made on this date from D.F. Malan Airport to Swartkop AFB. Although the type were officially retired from service on 23 November 1984, with a parade and flypast to mark the occasion.

Sgt G van den Berg   Ill-fated Avro Shackleton MR 3 serial 1716/J in happier times patrolling above the seas off Cape Town (*ad astra*)

Avro Shackleton serial 1722 ready for take-off *(ad astra)*

The MR. 3 variant was the only Shackleton equipped with a nose-wheel, which in RAF service, at one time proved to be the types Achilles heel with a number of nose-wheel collapses occurring, both on taxiing and touch down *(ad astra)*

32

Shackleton serial 1716 had been restored to airworthy condition by a dedicated team of retired SAAF personnel at the air force museum at Ysterplaat outside Cape Town. It was due to take part in the July 1994, Flying Legends Display at the Duxford Imperial War Museum airfield in the UK and the RAF Benevolent Fund's International Air Tattoo at RAF Fairford, Gloucestershire, later in the same month.

Leading the team on its visit to the UK was Project and Liaison Officer Major Horace Blok, an experienced navigator. The airplane was flown by Major 'Pine' Pienaar with Major Peter Dagg as co-pilot. In addition to the normal crew of thirteen, for this epic long-range flight a small team of specialist aircraft technicians were also on board. It left Cape Town on 7 July that year on the first leg of its 35-hour journey including stopovers at Libreville and Abidjan. It had encountered engine problems at Abidjan, but having cleared these, it took-off for the long slog to Lisbon. Near to the border with Morocco it began losing power in two engines, as a consequence the crew were forced to carry out an emergency wheels-up landing close to the Mauritanian/Western Sahara border, shortly after 01.30 hours on the morning of 13 July. All nineteen on board were uninjured and rescued by helicopter to fly back to South Africa, but the Shackleton was abandoned in the desert with a severely distorted airframe.

Probably the most infamous Shackleton *Pottie's Bomber* of the SAAF fleet is serial 1722 which after restoration by a team of technicians led by Warrant Officer 'Pottie' Potgeiter, was flown back to Ysterplaat on 6 December 1991, to be maintained in pristine condition by the SAAF Museum Ysterplaat Branch. This particular airplane was involved in a dramatic rescue mission on 30 October 1965, to locate the crew of a Blackburn Buccaneer S.50 serial 417 of No.24 Squadron which ditched in the Atlantic Ocean near Ascension Island during its delivery flight. The crew were found by Shackleton 1722, who dropped them a ten man dinghy and after spending some thirteen hours in the water they were picked up by a passing ship, the Dutch registered freighter *Randfontein.*

The only overseas order for the Buccaneer was for sixteen airplanes for the SAAF, the order signed in October 1962. Based on the S.2 variant, a pair of Bristol Siddeley BS605 rocket engines were installed in the rear fuselage for hot-and-high operations and it was designated S.50. The rockets generated 35.6kN (8,000 lb) of thrust between them and, together with the two Rolls-Royce Mk 101 Speys, produced over 133.4kN (30,000 lb) of s.t. The first SAAF Buccaneer S.50 was flown on 9 January 1965, and deliveries to RAF Lossiemouth, Scotland, where crews were converted to type, commenced in May, 1965. The first eight were ferried by air to South Africa in two batches of four airplanes, departing the UK on 27 October, 1965. They landed at Waterkloof AB on 6 November, having lost serial 417 en-route 500 miles south of the Cape Verde Islands. As a result of the policy of apartheid in existence in South Africa at the time, the British Labour Government of the day refused to sanction delivery of an attrition replacement and a follow-on order of at least another sixteen aircraft. As a result this was the last British-designed fixed-wing combat plane to be sold to South Africa.

The Buccaneers all served with No.24 Squadron, SAAF, and although procured as a maritime strike plane equipped with up to four Nord AS.30 air-to-surface missiles to defend the Cape sea routes, it also participated in many overland operations. Prior to their use in Angola, the SAAF Buccaneers conducted two strikes on floundering oil tankers, similar to the Fleet Air Arm attacks on the *Torrey Canyon,* to prevent coastal pollution, in March 1971 and April 1972.

Unlike the RAF's Buccaneers that did not make their combat debut until the Gulf War in 1991, No.24 Squadron's airplanes went to war several times well ahead of this. In September 1987, four Buccaneers were deployed from Waterkloof and used in support of ground forces in Angola, being based in northern South West Africa (now Namibia). In a period of 102 days, No.24 Squadron flew 99 sorties, including 32 multi-aircraft strikes, and dropped 701 bombs. These strikes were made in the face of an extensive Soviet SAM threats, both static and shoulder launched variants, AAA with quad 23mm cannon and interception by MiG-21 and MiG-23 Angolan Air Force fighters flown by Cuban and East German pilots.

The Angolan defence systems were supported by excellent Soviet supplied radar cover and the strikes were flown in extremely bad weather conditions with the approach below 30 metres (100 ft) to keep below the radar horizon. The first Buccaneer strike was flown on 7 September 1987, against Angola's 47 Brigade in the Lomba River area, in company with Mirage F.1AZs of No.1 Squadron. Ten 250 kg (551 lb) pre-fragmented bombs were dropped by each Buccaneer primarily using the 'long toss' technique that permitted the airplanes to remain outside the range of most of the Angolan air defences.

The success of these raids flown throughout September, October and November 1987, without loss, can be adjudged by the intercepted radio message sent by the Angolan ground commander after an attack by Buccaneers and Mirages on 26 September: "the aviation came through... we did not see them... everything is (destroyed)."

On 3 January 1988, No.24 Squadron's Buccaneers had the distinction of dropping the SAAF's first 'smart bomb', to take out the centre-span of the bridge at Cuito Cuanavale. The bomb destroyed 20m (66 ft) of the bridge and damaged a similar distance either side. The strike was flown in spite of a number of Angolan Air Force MiG-23s in the area. Two of the Buccaneers were actually locked onto by the MiGs who did not engage them. Despite this the Buccaneer did have a very high attrition rate in SAAF service and sanctions placed a strain on the Atlas Aircraft Corporation to support the remaining airplanes. When the type was finally withdrawn from service on 30 June 1991, as part of a force rationalisation and a diminished operational need with the Bush wars at an end, only five remained.

The only other pure bomber type operated by the SAAF at this time were the six English Electric Canberra B (I) Mk 12 and three Mk.4 trainers ordered in 1962. The bombers arrived in South Africa in 1963 and 1964, to be used by No.12 Squadron as tactical bombers and on high-altitude reconnaissance duties. No.12 Squadron at Waterkloof, flew its last Canberra sortie on 30 November, 1990. The remaining five B(I) 12s were sold to Peru and left for South America on 17 December, 1991. The one remaining flyable T Mk 4 followed in early 1995.

No.12 Squadron's first combat operations on type were flown on 4 May 1978, following a prolonged period of reconnaissance sorties over Angola and the west coast and up the east coast towards Maputo, in Mozambique. As the Soviets sought to promote the communist doctrine throughout the Third World by supplying military aid to client states' to support local conflicts, to further de-stabilise the region, early in 1978, it was decided that a significant threat to South Africa existed, and action was needed. The raid on the guerrilla bases at Cassinga in Angola mounted by No. 12 Squadron's Canberras and No.24 Squadron's Buccaneers that began on the night of 3/4 May 1978, was the most complex military operation ever mounted by the South African Defence Force and was based on techniques first developed by NATO for use within the Central European Theatre. By this time in SAAF service, the original Canberras task of interdictor/bomber had largely been replaced by deploying the airplane in the photo-recce role as the types uprated R-R Avon 109 engines bestowed the bomber with a high-level radius of action both at high and low altitudes, as was well suited to the vast distances to be covered in the region. But, for this operation No.12 Squadron crews had been trained in tactical low-level work using the precision techniques developed for the B.6 and B(I)8 Canberra interdictor variants used by the RAF in Germany.

No. 24 Squadron Buccaneers and No. 12 Squadron Canberra bombers devoid of all markings prepare for the raid on Cassinga guerrilla bases in Angola. *(SAAF)*

Four airplanes had been prepared for the mission, with their extensive reconnaissance suite normally fitted, removed, on this occasion instead, the bomb-bay full of 'Alpha' weapons resembling giant billiard balls. Released from dispensers in sequence these bombs first developed by the Americans for use in Vietnam, on release would cover an area of around 100m x 800m (330 ft x 2,625 ft) bounced on landing, exploding at around 6 metres (20 ft) such that the blast would incapacitate anything or anyone in its immediate vicinity. It was planned to deliver these from line abreast formation at an altitude of 152 metres (500 ft) and 360 knots. Earlier photographic reconnaissance missions of the target area revealed gunpits, miles of zig-zag trenches and star-shaped concrete pads characteristic of those WarPact missile defence sites deployed by the Eastern bloc in Europe. It was obvious surprise would be of the essence.

The mission was to test the crews training and competence to the limit, the operation being rather more complex than simulated in any previous training. Involving a night, weapons, no-radio departure, high-level silent transit, let-down over unmapped enemy terrain, low-level penetration to undertake a precision strike on a heavily defended target, and a low-level recovery to an away base. One of the squadron's aircrew had flown around 1,000 hours on Canberras, but most had logged only about 100 hours and most were about to double their night flying hours on type. In addition nobody had told them just how difficult the mission would likely to be.

The airplanes took off one after the other and settled into a loose formation for the long night transit high above the Kalahari Desert. The cabins were cold and icy and frost grew thick on the frames from exhaled breath. Pilots under the bombers offset canopies shuffled their feet in an effort to keep warm. While the navigator bomb/aimers were hunched over their plotting tables in the long nose. As the second phase of the mission unfolded - the 320 km (200 mile) low-level penetration - the navigators moved forward glad to stretch their limbs after crouching for hours, to settle in the prone position in the Perspex nose behind the Pitot tube and the visual bomb-sight. At 07.45 hours the four bombers, now in tight formation are on track with ten seconds in hand after flying some 1,770km (1,100 miles) at night, in complete radio silence, over virtually featureless terrain to spray their 720 Alpha weapons on the target at precisely 08.00 hours. Only three seconds late, all weapons were on target and No.12 Squadron - *Primus in Acien* - was already flying a tactical departure. Behind them No.24 Squadron Buccaneers were now running in to unload salvos of 454kg (1,000 lb) iron bombs onto the WarPac-style hardpoints and just three minutes away with an insertion force of 500 paratroops were a fleet of SAAF C-130 Hercules and C-160 Transall transports flying in groups of four, in a low-level racetrack formation ready to commence the biggest operational para-drop since Arnhem in WW II. All co-ordinated by the On-Scene Commander Airborne (OSCA) in a Douglas DC 4 Skymaster.

No. 44 Squadrons Douglas DC. 4 in low-viz camouflage were used as staff transports and airbourne command post in the Angolan War. *(SAAF)*

Still reeling from the totally unexpected devastating attack on their complex a number of the surviving 2,500 defenders of the guerrilla base tried to co-ordinate some resistance. But, despite some heavy resistance using AAA and heavy weapons they were overcome and the base over-run by 09.30 hours. As mopping up operations began, No.24 Squadron's Buccaneers, who were still circling the area, spotted a small column of armoured vehicles emerging from a small police post attached to a farming community about 24 km (15 miles) away. This small but efficient force of light tanks, armoured fighting vehicles (AVFs), and trucks full of infantry, were heading at great speed towards the action.

Realising this had all the hallmarks of a potential disaster for the lightly-armed paratroops, unless the column was stopped by an air strike, the OSCA dispatched three of the Buccaneers to re-arm at a base in adjacent South West Africa, where some of No.24 Squadron's ground-crew had deployed to provide engineering back-up. Luckily these also had a few rocket packs not called for in operational orders but taken along 'just in case'. Low on fuel and with not much ammunition one Buccaneer remained behind to take on the column. It succeeded in 'taking out' several of the AVFs, forcing the column to leave the road on a number of occasions. By the time the three other strike bombers returned after completing the fastest engine-running turnaround in history - the lone 'Bucc' having expended all its ammunition was reduced to making low-level noisy passes over the column which was still edging its way towards the smoke at Cassinga, in spite of the renewed attacks by the returning Buccaneers.

Fortunately, whilst this unplanned action was taking place, the OSCA had advanced his Extraction Plan by several hours, and it was not long before a force of Puma and Super Frelon helicopters that had been leap-frogging north for several days, were on hand to set up a shuttle to ferry the paras and sacks of captured documents out to a makeshift landing ground. A number of the helicopters needing to divert to ferry additional fuel to the temporary holding ground. At the same time, the remnants of the armoured column realising the limitations of the opposition, began to get bolder and continued to move forward, the best the Buccaneers could do now, was to slow them to allow the helicopters to do their job. Luckily just as some additional Cuban and East German RPVs arrived from the south the last Puma helicopter struggled into the air and with the Skymaster banked away to safety. No.12 Squadron's Canberras, that by this time had rearmed and stood at cockpit readiness on AFB Grootfontein, in Namibia, were stood down. All the Buccaneers recovered safely to their FOB and not one helicopter was lost. There were only three paratrooper fatalities. It is estimated by leading defence analysts from more than one continent that this amazing attack mounted by the SAAF's Southern Strike Force, set the Soviets plans for de-stabilisation of the region back by at least a year.

A 'lone' Buccaneer of the Southern Strike Force returns to base. *(SAAF)*

In concluding our earlier brief review of No. 35 Squadron's Avro Shackleton operations it is reported in the squadron diary that serial 1722 was fortunate on one occasion to survive its own ditching. On a landing approach at Langgebaanweg AFB (approximately 100 miles north of Capetown), the nose-wheel refused to lock down. After many unsuccessful attempts by the crew to rectify the situation with the main gear locked and not retractable almost six hours after the problem was first noticed preparations were made for a crash landing. All moveable weight was shifted to the rear of the airplane and foam was spread on the runway to reduce the friction of the nose on the tarmac. As 1722 touched down at 40 knots the nose dropped to the tarmac, the airplane eventually sliding to a standstill. None of the crew were injured and the airplane suffered only minimal damage.

The United Nations embargo against South Africa and its policy of apartheid, forced the SAAF to 'make do' with the airplanes it had. The SAAF was, therefore, the first and last operator of the Shackleton MR.3. With no access to authorised replacement parts, these had to be manufactured locally, anything was made from air coolers, radiator cores, connecting rods, seals and gaskets and hundreds of other parts, with parts often 'borrowed' from airplanes on deep servicing to keep others in the air. All seven airplanes were completely rewired in 1978, and two were later stripped and re-sparred in 1984. Nevertheless, on 23 November 1984, after 27 years of excellent service and with more than 30,000 hours of flying time recorded, the SAAF were forced to withdrawn the type from use due to the mainspars having not sufficient flying hours. With the United Nations embargo making it impossible for the air force to purchase a creditable replacement, it was forced to adapt No.27 Squadron's Piaggio P.166S Albatross airplanes which had been acquired for inshore patrol in 1969 (and subsequently retired in November 1990), for the maritime patrol role. No. 35 Squadron was, therefore, subsequently re-equipped with the veritable Douglas C-47 (Maritime) Dakota transport.

The first SAAF Dakotas were based in the Union from late 1945, transporting South African military personnel home from the European War. The SAAF had been operating the type since June 1943, with a total of 58 on inventory at one time, flying principally from southern Africa to North Africa and then in the Mediterranean theatre from Italy. Operating under the control of No.5 Wing the two founder squadrons were Nos. 28 and 44. No.28 Squadron returned home with more than twenty Dakotas on charge in October, 1945, to continue repatriating South African nationals from Europe and undertake general flying duties at home. A large number of surplus Dakotas appeared on the market and some were transferred to South African Airways, the survivors appearing back on the SAAF's inventory in 1971.

In 1948, SAAF Dakotas took on a new role when No.60 Squadron operated them for two years on a nationwide aerial survey. Meanwhile, by 1963, No.28 Squadron had given up most of its Dakotas to replace them with the Lockheed C-130B Hercules. But the cavernous, noisy 'Herk' was not best suited for VIP duties and a handful of Dakotas were kept on No.28 Squadrons inventory until 1968, when all VIP duties became the premise of No.21 Squadron. The 'Daks' supplanted two years later when four HS.125-400B named *Mercurius* (the Afrikaans rendering of Roman - "message of the Gods"), in SAAF service, took over the duties. Among many other variations the "Stock Scheme C" HS 125s, were equipped to launch underwing rockets, though their primary role was VIP transport. Quite unbelievably three of them (01, 02, and 03), in good visibility were lost on the 26 May 1971, when they flew into Devils Peak, Cape Town, while taking part in a rehearsal for the 1971 Republic Day Celebrations. Three replacements were ordered and these arrived in 1972. A further HS/BAe 125 (ZS-LME) was delivered in September, 1983. The three remaining 125s were finally retired in 1999, after more than twenty-five years service.

When the sanctions were imposed on the country in the mid-1970s, a number of Dakotas were purchased from various sources to supplement those still in SAAF service. In total sixteen were added to the air arms inventory and most were allocated "old" serials. One of the most 'interesting' purchases was the five ex-RNZAF Dakotas which were withdrawn from use by that service in 1977. These airplanes were purchased by an organisation in the Comores, with the name Island Associates and given Comores registration before delivery. Once they had arrived safely in the Comores, they were soon flown on to South Africa where they were given "old" serials in the SAAF numbering system. Their relatively low hours, has seen some of these converted into the C-47TP "Turbo Dak" programme.

These, and other acquisitions meant, by the early 1980s there were three main Dakota units in the SAAF battle order, as well as a number of squadron 'hacks'. No. 25 Squadron was at Ysterplaat for maritime patrol work, No.44 at Swartkop on general duties and a training unit, No.86 Multi-Engine Flying School (MEFS) at Bloemspruit. Most Dakotas at this time were used to support the operations in South West Africa against SWAPO (South West Africa People's Organisation) insurgents up to the peace settlement of 1989.

In 1984, with the demise of the Avro Shackleton it was the piston-engined Douglas C-47 Dakota that assumed the maritime duties of No.35 Squadron at its base at D. F. Malan Airport. Six years later in November 1990, the unit absorbed No.25 Squadrons airplanes to become a mixed role squadron assuming responsibility for maritime patrol, general transport, target towing and navigator training!

Today (2003), the SAAF is still the largest operator of the veritable Douglas C-47 Dakota, albeit, in its C-47TP incarnation. Most of which (8), are operated by No.35 Squadron at D.F Malan Airport in the maritime patrol role. The Turbo Dak is not simply a 'stop gap' airplane the conversion at a stroke afforded the SAAF with a 'zero-time' airframe well suited for its task. The stretched twin-turbine Dakleton is equipped with the latest avionics, radar and radio equipment. It can carry over 4,000 lb more payload; seven more passengers; climb at twice the rate; cruise at 35 knots faster and fly nearly 500 miles more than its piston-engined cousin. The Dakleton is fitted with a comprehensive radar/navigation system and the rear fuselage has been modified to take a battery of smoke canisters and flares, which can by ejected from a series of chutes in the under-fuselage. A 10-man air droppable life-raft is the main rescue accessory carried, although in most cases it is the Dakletons primary task when on air-sea-rescue duties, to locate the subject, assist if needed, while directing surface or rotary-wing rescue assets to the scene.

Lt RP Raubenheimer   No. 35 Squadrons 'Super' Daks at rest in the Cape Town sunset *(ad astra)*

3. Bush Wars

War had become a way of life in Angola long before Portugal granted the country its independence in November 1975. Formed in 1958, a low-key threat also existed from South West Africa (now Namibia) that in 1960, established a formalised military unit - the People's Liberation Army of Namibia (PLAN) as Angola plunged itself into a civil war. The internal conflict in Angola involved three main factions, the one of greatest concern was the Marxist *Movimento Popular de Libertacao de Angola* (MPLA) who were supplied by the USSR and who were receiving massive numbers of Cuban 'advisers'. With the withdrawal of the Portuguese, in January 1976, the MPLA quickly established the *Force Aerea Populaire de Angola/Difesa Anti-Avioes* (Angolan People's Air Force/ Anti-Aircraft Defence) with some of the airplanes abandoned by the Portuguese Air Force and eight MiG-21MFs supplied by the Soviet Union. Moscow quickly stepped up the supply of arms and aircraft, and more MiG-21MFs were air freighted into the country. As well as arms and airplanes, large numbers of Russians, East Germans and Cubans entered the country to bolster the Angolan armed forces.

From 1966 to 1989, the SAAF was involved in the Bush War in South West Africa (Namibia) and later Angola. Making extensive use of its locally-designed Cheetahs on combat missions. A United Nations resolution against selling arms to South Africa in the mid-1960s lead to it turning to France for its aircraft and later a number of Kfirs were purchased from Israel. After a later complete embargo on arms sells these aircraft were modified and updated locally by Atlas, who were later to produce a number of completely "new build" aircraft. These aircraft were designated "Cheetah.". These highly modified and developed Mirages now (2004) form the SAAFs main combat type. Another locally developed type is the Oryx helicopter, an upgrade of the Aerospatiale Puma. Other new types to have entered SAAF service include the Boeing B.707 tanker/transports two of which have IAI Phased-Array radar fitted, giving airborne early-warning capability.

From 1975, the Republic of South Africa (RSA) assisted in a major incursion into Angola - Operation *Savannah* to support anti-MPLA forces. At this time SAAF support was limited to helicopter, transport and reconnaissance operations, until the South African forces pulled out in January 1976. Although, as the PLAN's activities in South West Africa began to escalate, in May 1978, the SAAF was called into action to support RSA ground forces in Operation *Reindeer* and pre-emptive ground strikes were made by the SAAF's Southern Strike Force on two PLAN bases within Angola. By 1980, the SAAF were regularly overflying Angolan territory, not only for reconnaissance, but also to undertake precision strikes against PLAN installations. As Soviet military aid continued backed by an ever increasing Cuban presence, Angola's military (*Forca Arma Populaire de Liberacione Angola* - FAPLA) began to establish a sophisticated air defence of Soviet equipped SAM sites complete with radar and control sites, backed up with comprehensive anti-aircraft artillery (AAA).

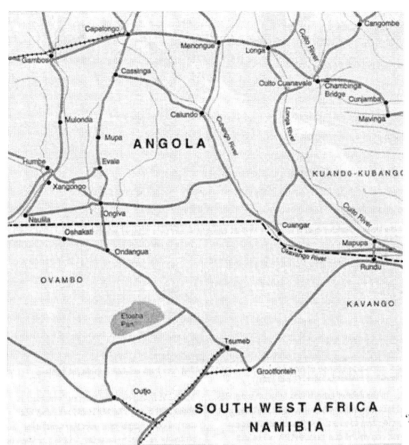
'Bush War' territory. *(MAP)*

Sgt V Vallentgoed

United Nations Soviet-built Mil Mi-8 utility helicopter used in Angola
for a number of years without mishap or major servicing *(ad astra).*

As the FAPLA's air defence system continued to expand, by 1979, the SAAF deployed regular detachments of its fleet of 100 Atlas Impala II (licence-built Aermacchi MB.326Ks) single-seat light ground-attack planes at Mpacha and Ondangwa. The type serving with distinction in the border war against the PLAN insurgents. SAAF Impala II strike planes destroyed six Angolan Air Force (FAPA) Soviet-built Mil helicopters in two sorties in September and October 1985, effectively bringing to an end the massive Russian-backed and supplied Operation *Second Congress* which had been launched to cripple Dr Jonas Savimbi's Inita movement. The Angolans never used their helicopters again during Operation *Second Congress*. Except their French-built Alouettes to pull all the Russian advisers out of the front-line positions when the South Africa ground forces threatened to overrun FAPLA positions. This was the first time in history that an Impala light ground-attack plane, developed from the Macchi MB.326B jet trainer had destroyed enemy airplanes in aerial combat.

Around 151 dual-seat licence-built Atlas Impala I (Aermacchi MB 326M) were used for jet flying training, supplementing the piston-engined North American Harvard basic trainer introduced into service in WW II. Following the introduction of the Impala I in 1966, this type was used by the SAAF's official aerobatics team the 'Silver Falcons', the Harvard Aerobatic Team disbanding in 1965. However, the Harvards did make a come-back in 1985, giving their final performance at their retirement ceremony held at Langebaanweg on 17 November, 1995. The team flying a 'Missing Man' formation.

The first three Harvards (NA-60s) were delivered to South Africa in February 1940, after a Lend-Lease agreement was signed with the Royal Air Force. Following evaluation with No.6 and No.10 SAAF Squadrons, the airplanes were transferred to 62 Air School (Central Flying School) at Temple. A fourth Harvard was delivered shortly afterwards being used as a technical training airframe. These initial deliveries were allocated SAAF serials 1301-1304. Subsequently the RAF and SAAF agreed to establish a Joint Air Training Scheme (JATS) in which South Africa would supply the ground facilities including hangars and fuel, while the RAF would supply the airplanes from their American Lend-Lease deliveries. Soon afterwards the SAAF announced that, it too, was to operate the Harvard as its advanced trainer to replace the two main training types then in use, the Hawker Hart and Miles Master which were becoming unreliable and suffering from overheating.

The first Harvard deliveries arrived in South Africa by sea from the United States in 1942, and then assembled at an air depot near the port. By 1944, 436 Mk.IIs, IIAs and Mk IIIs had been delivered, to meet the JATS needs and gradually replace the SAAF Harts and Masters. Local serials within the range 7001-7633 were allocated to these airplanes. Of the 633 Harvards received, 300 of the survivors were returned to the United States at the end of the war under the terms of the Lend-Lease scheme. Nine Mk IIAs were transferred to the Royal Navy early in 1945. Another 178 of both versions were returned to the RAF in the UK. A number of these were subsequently passed on to the air forces of Belgium, Denmark, Greece and Italy. Those Harvards remaining were taken on charge by the SAAF to equip the Central Flying School (CFS), the Operational Training School at Langebaanweg and the Auxiliary Squadrons. In 1947, twenty Harvards were dispatched to the Royal Netherlands Air Force, while another nine were sent to Southern Rhodesia.

Atlas Impala I used by the Silver Falcons aerobatic display team stream the national colours. *(ad astra)*

In 1951, Harvards were assigned to the new Citizen Force Squadrons which were attached to the training squadrons. But, there were insufficient airplanes available to fully equip these new units, prompting deliveries of an additional 65 refurbished ex-USAF and US Navy Texans in 1952, under the US Military Aid Program. These airplanes, modified to Mk IIA (AT-6C) standard, were serialled between 7634 and 7698, following on from the WW II allocations. Another thirty re-manufactured T-6Gs were obtained in 1953, within the serial range 7699-7728. The T-6G was designed for navigation training and was able to perform aerobatics or carry weapons. From 1975, the Harvards were replaced by Atlas Impalas in the Citizen Force Squadrons.

Despite their long lineage, SAAF Harvards performed tours of duty during the Border War, operating from Runtu on armed reconnaissance flights to support the Portuguese in southern Angola for a short time during August, 1967. Two years later the SAAF sold sixty Harvards to the Portuguese, who operated them in northern Angola. Harvards were also used for a number of short tours of duty in South West Africa (Namibia), and in 1976 were hastily camouflaged for use in Operation *Savannah* where they flew armed reconnaissance missions, although they did not cross into Angolan airspace or perform combat sorties. During its SAAF service the Harvard was utilised in various roles including light attack, weather reconnaissance and target towing, in addition to its primary duty of training student pilots.

In SAAF service the Harvard was mainly used as a primary trainer at the CFS, with most of the air arms pilots receiving their initial flying instruction on the type. The CFS formed at Zwartkop in 1932, and was relocated to Dunnottar in 1946, where it remained until the end of 1992, when it moved to Langebaanweg. The remaining Harvards continued to operate from here until their official retirement in 1995. During 1990, seventy airplanes, including around forty AT-6s, received an avionics upgrade under project name *Ice Cream* by No.4 Air Depot SAAF, to produce the locally designated Harvard Mk IV.

The main purpose of the upgrade was to allow for a smooth transition to the air arms new basic turbo-trainer still under evaluation at the time. As is now known, the final choice from a plethora of types available was the excellent Pilatus PC 7 Mk II, named 'Astra' in SAAF service.

The Air Force declared eighty-seven Harvards officially on strength in 1995, although it is believed more than ninety were still in service at this time. With more than sixty gathered at Langebaanweg for its retirement where the air force flew a formation flypast of 55 airplanes. The largest formation ever flown in South Africa, one for every year of service. One airplane, serial 7449, was placed as a memorial at the airfields main gate and the ten airplanes which did not receive the avionics refit were bequeathed to the Harvard Club. To be maintained in flying condition, six in the various colours schemes used between 1940-1995.

F/sgt PB Vermaak   The Harvard Display Team, with smoke on, heads out over the coast *(ad astra)*

The Harvards were finally replaced completely in 1996, with the Swiss Pilatus PC-7 Mk II 'Astra' Turbo Trainer. The Harvard aerobatics team giving its final display in October 1995, at the International Air Show at Waterkloof. The 'Astra' is fitted with Martin-Baker ejection seats under a locally designed and manufactured cockpit and is fitted with a high-powered Pratt & Whitney Canada PT6A engine driving a four-bladed propeller. The first batch of 60 were delivered in October 1994, by sea to Cape Town where they were taken by road to Ysterplaat AFB for assembly and test flying. They were then flown the short distance north to Langebaanweg to join the CFS in late in 1994. In late 1995, sufficient Astras had arrived for the Harvard to be officially retired. By the beginning of 1996, forty-four had been delivered to permit the first intake of student pilots to commence training on type in April 1996. Two airplanes were assigned to the SAAF Test and Development Centre at Bredasdorp. With 58 remaining on inventory in 2002, it is planned to reduce the total Astra complement to just forty airplanes. Astra is now the mount of the famous 'Silver Falcons Display Team'.

85 AFS Atlas Impala I
(ad astra)

The Atlas Impala fleet (18 IIs and 30 Is) are to be partly replaced by twenty-four dual-seat BAe Hawk 100 LIFT (Lead-In Fighter Trainers) between 2005-2009, with the Impala fleet reducing to twenty-four airplanes. It is understood the Hawks, most of which will be licence manufactured locally by Denel/Atlas Aircraft as part of an offset agreement, will be based at Louis Trichadt AFB in a single squadron. The first BAE Systems, SAAF Hawk is scheduled to fly at Brough in the UK, in March 2003.

The CFS new mount is the customised Swiss Pilatus PC 7 II 'Astra' *(ad astra)*

On 1 November 1981, in an effort to stop SWAPO terrorist from crossing the border into South West Africa No.3 Squadrons Dassault Mirage F.1CZ made their operational debut, during Operation *Daisy. Daisy* lasted for twenty days. Its primary objective was to strike hard at the heart of Angola and make the SWAPO fighters understand that they could find no sanctuary in the area. Less than a week into the operation, as the South African Army cleared away SWAPO camps and destroyed vast amounts of ammunition and equipment, the Angolan Air Force deployed its MiG-21s over the area. The first MiG incursion over the area was detected at 07.00 hours on 6 November by the radars at Ondangwa Air Base where two No.3 Squadron Mirage F.1CZs were standing ready for QRT (Quick Reaction Take-off).

Maj F Naudé   Two No. 3 Squadron Mirage F.1CZs head out on another sortie into Angolan airspace *(ad astra)*

Immediately the two Mirage single-seat interceptors one piloted by Major Johann Rankin, and the other by his wingman Captain du Plessis took-off and transited at a very low-level to avoid the Angolan radars to the position the MiGs were detected. Climbing to 7,620 metres (25,000 ft) Plessis spotted the MiGs and the Mirages dropped their external fuel takes in order to make a tight turn to get behind the Angolan fighters, that were flying in formation into the sun. For this reason the Mirage pilots decided not to use their Armscor-developed V3 Kikri heat-seeking guided missiles in case they should lock onto the sun instead of the MiGs. Major Rankin fired a burst of explosive shells and one of the MiGs started leaking aviation fuel at the same time breaking to the left with Rankin in pursuit. Captain Plessis followed the other MiG who went off to the right-hand side. As Rankin continued to close on his MiG at about 500m (1,640 ft) he opened fire again with his cannons. The MiG exploded breaking into two pieces. As Rankin looked for his wingman he saw the MiG pilot's parachute about 3,000 metres (10,000 ft) below. At the same time the Mirages were warned that other MiGs were on their way to the sector, and Rankin called to his wingman to break away from his engagement with the second MiG to return to base at Ondangwa. Having recorded No.3 Squadron's first air victory since the Korean war, thirty years earlier, somewhat surprising some of the SAAF "top brass" were not so enthused as they feared an escalation in Angolan air activity might end in reprisal involving many intensive air battles to a numerically superior force. They were well aware that following the initial deliveries of MiG-21s further examples had been delivered as well as a squadron of MiG-17 fighter-bombers, twenty-three more up-to-date MiG-23s, ten Sukhoi Su-22s, 42 Mil Mi-8 and Mi-17 transport helicopters and twenty-five Mil Mi-25 Hind attack helicopters.

Coincidentally, nearly a year later, on 5 October 1982, Major Rankin was again involved in a dogfight with an Angolan MiG-21. Together with his wingman Captain Cobus Toerien, the two Mirages were escorting a No.12 Squadron Canberra on a reconnaissance mission over the SWAPO bases. Flying at 6,100 metres (20,000 ft) South African radars warned the two Mirage pilots Angolan MiGs were on their way to intercept them. Immediately, the Mirages climbed to 9,100 metre (30,000 ft) and No.12 Squadrons Canberra was sent back to Ondangwa.

At altitude Major Rankin spotted the two MiGs approaching in the two o'clock position. Both Mirages dropped their external tanks and continued to approach the MiGs head on. As soon as the MiG pilots spotted the SAAF interceptors they released their infra-red guided Atoll missiles which failed to lock-on to their targets. The MiGs continued to fly on past the Mirages who executed a 180° turn to try to catch them. Having locked their Aïda ranging radars on to the two MiGs the Mirages accelerated to Mach 1.3 and at about 1,500 metres (4,900 ft) Rankin fired an Armscor V3B Kukri air-to-air missile which exploded close to the MiG. The MiG, although controllable was badly damaged and unable to lower its landing gear and its fuselage was badly scraped when it was forced to make a belly landing. Moving in on the second MiG, Rankin flew right in on the airplane to within just 300 metres (980 ft) before opening fire, the MiG exploded and Rankin flew through the ball of fire with his F.1. As in the 1981 interception, Major Rankin was convinced that the MiG pilot was Cuban. Later, South African military intelligence confirmed his presumption was correct. What became obvious to the SAAF at this time was whether Angolan, Cuban or Russian the MiG pilots flew their airplanes to a rigid operational doctrine, that left little room for individual initiative. Ground control appeared to play a very important part in their attack techniques and while it was obvious some were more talented flyers than others, they all reacted in a more or less similar manner when engaged in aerial combat.

After the engagement the SAAF published a press statement announcing the destruction of a MiG in combat above Angola. As usual the Angolans responded with their own version of events. According to them, the MiGs successfully chased three SAAF airplanes and during a short battle a MiG was slightly damaged. The spokesman for the SAAF had the last word when he retorted the Angolan press statement was a "pathetic attempt to hide defeat".

At this time the SAAF made no secret or any attempt to hide the fact that they were making regular incursions into Angolan airspace. According to the then Minister of Defence, Magnus Malan, the SAAF reconnaissance flights were seen as an operational necessity in the constant hide-and-seek warfare employed by SWAPO and the South African security forces in charge of the protection of South West Africa's northern borders. The battles of 1981 and 1982 were the only occasion when Dassault Mirage F.1 airplanes and Soviet MiG-21s were engaged in air combat. They were also the only clashes between the South Africans and the Cuban-Angolan forces that ended in victory. During this period Major (later Colonel) Rankin flew fifty combat missions in Mirage F.1CZs. Between 1984 and 1986 he commanded the Jet Flying Training School based at Langebaanweg, returning to front-line duties with No.1 Squadron in 1986 to fly the Mirage F.1AZ variant, completing a further 70 combat missions during the ongoing war in Angola.

The ground-attack Mirage F.1AZ , entered service with No.1 Squadron early in 1976, based initially at Waterkloof AB. In January 1981, all the F.1AZs were moved to the ultra-modern base at Hoedspruit in the eastern Transvaal 45km (90 miles) from the Mozambique border. As the SAAF's premier squadron No.1 distinguished itself during operations from South West Africa (Namibia) into Angola. The squadron actually penetrated with relative impunity probably what at the time was the most heavily defended and sophisticated air defence environment in the world. During these missions the squadron had more than 100 SAMs launched against them. Many squadron pilots were awarded commendations for their courageous flying on these highly dangerous missions. Unfortunately despite their obviously superior equipment, training and tactics, political constraints prevented the SAAF from going on to deliver a final blow and finish it.

In any case, in reality there were not many air-to-air combats with the Angolan airplanes deep inside the country, as without in-flight refuelling support, it was necessary for the F.1AZ pilots to conserve as much fuel as possible while operating so far away from their base. Often having to travel long distances to the combat zone. One engagement between a Mirage F.1AZ and a MiG-23 ended in the MiG evading destruction, the air-to-air combat highlighting a problem with the Mirages equipment, that was promptly rectified in order to prevent any recurrence.

While the primary task allocated to No.1 Squadron was air-to-ground attack, in 1991, towards the end of the Angolan War, the dual primary and secondary air-to-air roles were undertaken when No.3 Squadrons F.1CZ interceptors were phased out of service. No. 3 Squadron disbanding in September, 1992. Currently (2003) the SAAF has twenty F.1AZs in its battle order, with No.1 'Billy Boys' Squadron still the custodians. It is understood a former WW II squadron commander would yell out "Jou Bielie", an Afrikaans compliment, to his pilots when they did something particularly outstanding. American pilots attached to the squadron at the time, misunderstood this as, "You Billies". From then on the squadron became known as the *Billy Boys,* assuming the 'Billy' callsign, the C.O. being *Billy* and the squadron members known as the *Boys.*

Although not in the same league as the F/A-18 Hornet or multi-role F-16 Fighting Falcon, the Mirage F.1AZ is more than adequate for the SAAF's ground-attack needs. Air superiority now being the sole premise of No.2 Squadrons Cheetahs based at Louis Trichardt. According to the F.1AZ pilots its DEFA 503 30mm cannon that can fire 1,200 rounds per minute is an extremely reliable and accurate weapon. The wing-tip missiles are the highly effective Armscor V3C manufactured in South Africa. Previously the airplane carried four pods of 72 rockets, but the increased use of 'smart' weapons made these redundant. Four Mk 82 bombs with a variety of fuses can also be carried under the fuselage with additional hardpoints provided for other stores. In addition to the weaponry, electronic warfare pods can be carried if necessary and chaff dispensers are also built into the housings below the tail-pipe. For long-distance sorties the F.1AZ has the option of two large fuel tanks — a third could be fitted under the fuselage if the bombs were not required.

No. 1 Squadron F.1AZ ground attack plane equipped with wing-tip AAM and full load of bombs *(ad astra)*

Two radar-equipped Mirage F-1CZs on 3 Squadrons dispersal at Waterkloof AB. *(ad astra)*

No. 1 Squadron low-viz Mirage F.1AZ with long-range tanks. Note white covered brake-chute housing and tail-fin RWR. *(ad astra)*

Having received its first delta-winged Dassault Mirage IIICZ in April 1963, in the early 1990s No.2 Squadron began conversion to the Mirage III South African upgrade, the Atlas Aviation Cheetah. Fifteen Mirage IIICZs were eventually delivered in 1963, followed by three dual-seat IIIBZ trainers in 1964. Subsequently the SAAF has flown numerous different types of the Dassault Mirage III. To supplement the Mirage IIICZ, seventeen IIIEZ front-line attack/interceptors were ordered and delivered during 1966, as well as three dual-seat IIIDZ trainers the following year, for 85 Air Combat School (ACS). A large number of these were ex-*Armée de l' Air* airplanes. For reconnaissance missions, four Mirage IIIRZs were ordered and delivered. These were fitted with a pack of five cameras specially positioned so that they could be focused in four different positions and for use at night. Later variants procured included eleven of the more powerful IIID2Z trainer as well as four IIIR2Z tactical reconnaissance aircraft. One (serial 856) was shot down in Angola on 6 July, 1979. Of the total 58 Dassault Mirage IIIs purchased by the SAAF, eight were written off in accidents and one was shot down in Angola.

Prompted partly by the strict United Nations embargo imposed in 1977, and by the realisation that the ageing Mirage III fleet was in need of refurbishment and modernisation, in the late 1970s the South African Cheetah programme was instigated to provide the SAAF with an effective strike fighter which could serve until at least the year 2000. The work to be undertaken locally by the Atlas Aircraft Corporation.

The first Cheetah (serial 845) to emerge was the 'D' variant, a two-seater which was evolved from the Mirage IIIDZ (2), IIID2Z (7) trainer, and five ex-IDF/AF Kfir 1s. The airplane appeared to be visually similar to the IAI Kfir-TC2 two-seat multi-role fighter with a slightly drooped nose (housing a dual-role Elta EL/M-2001B radar increasing its overall length slightly) and two manoeuvrability-enhancing fixed forward canards, dog tooth wing leading edge with increased camber and an in-flight refuelling probe. The Cheetah D fleet was initally flown in the summer of 1987, by 89 Combat Flying School (CFS) at Pietersburg AFB in the Cheetah conversion and tactical training roles. When that base closed in 1992, these airplanes were transferred to Louis Trichardt AFB where they joined their more advanced single-seat cousin, the Cheetah C, currently (2003) in use with No.2 Squadron.

The single-seat Cheetah E multi-role fighter followed the D model and was essentially an extensively re-modelled Mirage IIIEZ. Thirteen of the original seventeen examples delivered were converted to Cheetah E. Incorporating the Cheetah D external airframe (except for a 'bolt-on' in-flight refuelling probe) and wing modifications, the Cheetah E was further modified for solo management and operation, suitable for the air-to-air and air-to-surface roles. First delivered to the SAAF in 1988, the Cheetah E retained the original SNECMA Atar 09C engine of the Mirage IIIEZ which made them poor performers in their modified state. Subsequently, it was revealed the Cheetah E had only been intended as an interim airplane, and was withdrawn from service in 1993, and replaced with the Cheetah C.

A four-year R6.5 billion (£1.1 billion) programme ended in June 1995, with the delivery of the 38th and last Cheetah C to the SAAF. The Cheetah C representing a further upgrade of the basic Mirage III airframe. The main external changes from the Cheetah E is the reprofiled nose to take the new enhanced Elta EL 2032 radar, and the three-segment windscreen (see front cover) replaced with a one-piece unit giving its pilots unobscured vision. The Cheetah C programme was shrouded in great secrecy, but it is believed the airplanes are re-worked ex-IDF/AF Kfir C 10s fitted with an Atar 09K-50 turbojet. A batch of 38 airframes ordered in 1988 from Israel.

There is no doubt the Cheetah, has a number of limitations as a air superiority fighter but it is not scheduled to be replaced until 2012-2015, with tranche 2 and possibly tranche 3 Saab JAS39 Gripen multi-role airplanes. The multi-role Saab Gripen, armed with the latest BVR Meteor (Beyond Visual Range) air-to-air missile will afford the SAAF with a creditable air defence asset for use well into the 21st century.

BAe/Saab JAS 39 Gripen test-fires
BVR Meteor AAM *(Saab)*

The main improvement of the Cheetah C over other developed Mirage III types, is that, it is powered by the SNECMA Atar 9K50 engine also used in the Mirage F.1 developing 70.21 kN (15,785 lb) s.t. with afterburning. Compared to the old 09C engine which powered the Cheetah E the 9K50 gives the airplane almost 16% greater dry thrust, and almost 13% more thrust with afterburner at sea-level. Operationally this translates into a 10-20% shorter take-off run; time from take-off to 12,200 metres (40,000 ft) at Mach 1.8 cut from 8.2 to 4.8 minutes and time to make a 180° turn at 11,000 metres (36,000 ft) is halved from 2.1 minutes to 1.1 minutes. Even so, the Cheetah upgrade was centred mainly around the avionic systems. Despite the canards and the refined aerodynamics and additional power afforded by the 9K50 engine, the airplane is still basically a Mirage III. To quote Lt-Col Cobus Toerien a former No.2 Squadron commander, "all the new avionics and electronic warfare (EW) equipment turned the Cheetah C into a relatively heavy airplane. In other words, the aerodynamic gains compared to the old Mirage IIIs were balanced by increased weight."

Nevertheless the Cheetah Cs enhanced avionics and multi-function pulse Doppler radar, which is claimed to be superior in the air-to-air mode over the F-16As does provide the SAAF with a very creditable multi-role platform. The Cheetahs cockpit is equipped with a sophisticated Head Up Display (HUD) and the Hands on Throttle & Stick (HOTAS) system. The airplane is also believed to carry one of the world's most advanced Electronic Warfare (EW) suites. To quote Lt-Col Toerien again, "we can receive information or do active jamming. That means we can look after ourselves in operations, we do not need dedicated EW support airplanes. Moreover all the equipment is internal, which is a great advantage because for every pod you have to carry, you take away a weapons station." The airplane is equipped with nine external store stations (including five under the fuselage) and can carry up to ten 250kg (550 lb) bombs in a ground-attack configuration. This is less than the 14 bombs that can be carried by the Mirage F.1AZ but the Cheetah can deliver its stores with greater accuracy, using its much more sophisticated targeting system. As with the Mirage F.1AZ the Cheetahs are equipped with a laser range finder fitted under the nose. The Cheetah C can also deliver laser-guided weapons although it does not carry a designator. Target designation has to be done from either another airplane or the ground.

Dissimilar Air Combat Training (DACT) against the F.1, highlights the limitations of the original delta-winged Dassault Mirage III in air combat. Although the enhanced Cheetah C with it canards is more manoeuvrable, the conventional high-winged F.1 can maintain a high speed turn for much longer. Nonetheless, at high speed, in a straight line, the Cheetah is said to be a "combat pilot's dream", with good supersonic acceleration and very snappy roll response. It is reported at low speed, if properly handled, it will fly straight and level at 100 knots, stall turn at zero and 'pull through' from the very low heights due to the canard-enhanced pitch performance. According to the pilots, the Cheetah's heavy nose improves manoeuvrability at low speed as well. Although, it has a very high landing speed of 190 knots.

No. 2 Squadron multi-role Cheetah C on ground-attack mission. *(ad astra)*

President F. W. de Klerk's historic referendum, at the end of a long period of counter-insurgency warfare in SWA (Namibia), the end of the Angolan War, South Africa's new political stance, cuts in the local defence budget, and the run up to the elections in 1994, had a profound effect on the SAAF's inventory.

Lt General J. P. B. Loggerenberg, then the Chief of the Air Force (CAF), announced a series of changes that would create a leaner, more cost effective force better suited to meet its new tasks. Its mission, to supply professional and cost effective operational air capabilities and to be fast acting and versatile.

The changes started to come into effect during 1990, and from 1991, were overseen by Lt General James Kriel, the new CAF. Lt-Gen Loggerenberg's main proposal was that the SAAF fleet of 800 airplanes should be reduced to 450 airplanes by 1995. A considerable number of types were phased out of service and many squadrons disbanded. All the Mirage IIIs, with the exception of the Cheetah Es were withdrawn, together with the Mirage F.1CZ, Blackburn Buccaneers, EE Canberra, SA 321 Super Frelon, SA 330C Puma, Atlas Bosbok and Kudu, Transall C-160, Douglas Skymaster, and Piaggio P 166S Albatross. As well as some Aerospatiale Alouette IIIs, Douglas C-47 Dakotas and Atlas Impalas. Many of the squadrons disbanded including Nos, 1, 2 (Oct 1990), 3 (Sep 1992), 4 (Sep 1991), 5, 6, 7, 10, 12 (Nov 1990), 16 (Oct 1990), 22, 24 (Mar 1991), 25 (Oct 1990), 27 (Oct 1990), 30 (Nov 1991) and No. 40. As well as Citizen Force unit 4 Squadron operating Atlas Impala I & II from the general aviation airfield at Lanseria disbanded in late 1991, 81 Fighter Training School (FTS) and 84 Light Aircraft School (LAS). 84 LAS Cessna C.185s later re-allocated to No.42 Squadron in October, 1992.

Unlike their Franco-German counterparts SAAF C-160Z Transalls do not carry an in-flight refuelling probe. *(ad astra)*

Numerous air force bases were closed and depots were shut, including Pietersburg, Port Elizabeth and Potchefstroom, Klippan Control and Reporting Post, and 402 Aerodrome Maintenance Unit. The effect of the 'peace dividend' was, that the SAAF's main role was now envisaged as a humanitarian one to provide assistance throughout southern Africa. Only one front-line squadron was retained in each role, with more than one if the role was in the broader interests of the Republic.

The ending of apartheid and the Cold War, the integration of the 'independent' homelands (TVBC) equipment into the SAAF inventory and the White Paper on Defence in 1996, provided for a Defence Review the main aspects affecting the future of the SAAF approved in 1997. A number of options were put forward with regards to the recommended SAAF future force design. Of these, the review recommended Option 1 specifying the air arms future with regards to missions, categories and equipment.

It was recommended the Atlas CHS-2 Rooivalk should be procured to provide the ground forces with direct support, anti-tank capabilities and provide rapid support to parachute and special forces Brigades.

In 2003, these airplanes already equipped No.16 Squadron at Bloemspruit. The review acknowledged that it is desirable the SAAF should retain both medium (36) and light fighter planes (16), to provide for direct fighter operations to establish air superiority over the battle area and provide aerial support for the ground forces with the airplanes capable of interdiction of the battlefield and operations behind enemy lines. The medium and light fighter requirement have been met by procurement of the latest Saab JAS 39 Gripen multi-role interceptor and the combat-capable BAE Systems Hawk Mk 120 Advanced Fighter Trainer. It is planned twenty-eight Atlas Cheetah C will remain in use until 2012, by which time all the Saab JAS 39 Gripens will be operational.

Option 1 determined, that for aerial surveillance and to cover all aspects of modern electronic warfare and airspace control, the existing fleet of five Boeing B.707s are more than adequate, with two equipped for AEW duties and all providing a creditable in-flight refuelling and "force multiplier" capability. It determined there was also a requirement for up to sixteen light reconnaissance airplanes and a squadron of remotely piloted vehicles (RPVs) which are already on inventory, and stored.

No. 60 Squadron Boeing 707-328 in-flight refuelling tanker before IAI ELINT/SIGINT conversion. Seen at the International Air Tattoo RAF Fairford, UK circa 1995 *(author)*

Air mobility, air transport needs would require an estimated forty-four fixed wing airplanes for medium and long-range transport duties and up to 96 transport helicopters, for troop transport, medium and heavy lift and casualty evacuation. Nine staff transports, government and VIP airplanes are required. In this respect, with only ten Lockheed C-130s and four C-160 Transalls in use and fifty Atlas Oyrx medium lift helicopters, the SAAF's air mobility assets fall well short of estimated requirements. Except, that is, the VIP fleet of seven airplanes.

South Africa's geographical position and its long coastline demands that in addition to those types already mentioned, that the air force retains a creditable maritime patrol capability. Airplanes that can patrol beyond the maritime defence areas, to provide an outer layer of defence by providing early warning, tracking and control capabilities. Option 1 determined, six new long-range and ten short-range maritime patrol planes were required.

In 2003, this requirement is met by the eight Dakletons of No.35 Squadron which no doubt will soldier on well into the decade and beyond. But it cannot be too long before the SAAF will be forced to seek a suitable replacement type for these rejuvenated WW II vintage Dakota transports. Corrosion is always a problem with maritime patrol airframes, similar to that which was discovered with the ex-US Navy Hercules (2) delivered to supplement the Hercules transport fleet. Shipborne maritime requirements have already been met by the order for four AgustaWestland Super Lynx 300 helicopters.

F/sgt PB Vermaak

An Atlas Kudu light observation plane on 'up country' patrol *(ad astra)*

SAAF Battle Order —- Circa August 1992: (Post-Restructuring and Rationalisation)

Unit	Equipment	Base
No. 1 Squadron	Mirage F.1AZ	Hoedspruit
No. 3 Squadron	Mirage F.1CZ	Waterkloof
No. 5 Squadron	Atlas Cheetah E	Louis Trichardt
No. 7 Squadron	Atlas Impala I & II	Langebaanweg
No. 8 Squadron	Atlas Impala I & II	Bloemspruit
No. 15 Squadron	Alouete III	Durban (Louis Botha Airport)
No. 17 Squadron	Alouette III, SA 330 Puma	Swartkop
No. 19 Squadron	SA 330 Puma, Atlas Oryx	Louis Trichardt
No. (VIP) 21 Squadron	HS-125-400B, Cessna C.550 Citation, Falcon 50 Falcon 900	Waterkloof (Pretoria)
No. 22 Squadron	Alouette III, SA 330 Puma	Ysterplaat (Cape Town)
No. 28 Squadron	C-130B Hercules, C-160Z Transall	Waterkloof
No. 31 Squadron	SA 330 Puma, Atlas Oryx	Hoedspruit
No. 35 Squadron	Douglas C-47B-35-DK Dakota (4), C-47TP	D.F. Malan (Cape Town)
No. 41 Squadron	Cessna C.208 Caravan I	Waterkloof
No. 42 Squadron	Atlas AM-3CM Bosbok (withdrawn Sept 1992) Cessna C.185A/D/E (from October 1992)	Pochefstroom Swartkop (Pretoria)
No. 44 Squadron	Douglas C-47 Dakota, C-47TP, Douglas DC-4 (5), Douglas C-54A (3) retired end 92	Swarkop - squadron moved to Waterkloof at the end of 1992.
No. 60 Squadron	Boeing B.707-328	Waterkloof
Central Flying School (CFS)	North American Harvard	Dunnottar
83 Jet Flying School (JFS)	Atlas Impala I	Langebaanweg
85 Combat Flying School (CFS)	Atlas Impala II	Pietersburg
86 Multi-Engined Flying School	Douglas C-47 Dakota	Bloemspruit (Bloemfontein)
87 Advanced Flying School (AFS)	C.185s until Oct 92, Alouette III (HFS)	Bloemspruit (Bloemfontein)
89 Combat Flying School (CFS)	Atlas Cheetah D	Pieterburg (later Louis Trichardt - No. 5 Sqdn)

Cessna C.185s replaced the Atlas Bosbok on front-line duties in October 1992 with No. 42 Squadron *(ad astra)*

4. The Helicopters

At its peak, the SAAF had six helicopter squadrons in its battle order, with sixty-three Aerospatiale SA 316/319 Alouette IIIs (some armed), and sixty-three SA 330 Puma tactical transports on front-line duties, as well as, thirty SE 3130 and seven SA 316 Alouette IIIs on training duties.

The first helicopters to appear in the SAAF battle order, were three Sikorsky S-51 Dragonflys in 1948. Initially they were used extensively against a plague of tsetse fly in Northern Zululand. Two of the early deliveries (A2 and A3) were lost in the region in 1952 and 1951 respectively. Sikorsky S-51 (A1) was subsequently restored by No.17 Squadron and is retained in non-flying condition by the SAAF Museum at Swartkop.

The next rotary-wing asset to be procured were three Sikorsky S-55s (A4, A5 and A6) in 1956/57. Allocated to No.17 Squadron they were deployed mainly on rescue duties both over the sea off Cape Town as well as inland mountain regions. These were followed by seven Aerospatiale Alouette II delivered in 1960. These were operated by No.17 Squadron at Ysterplaat Air Force Base near Cape Town mainly to train rotary-wing pilots, to fly the larger Alouette III 'Aylos' that began to arrive in the mid-1960s. As more and more Alouette IIIs arrived No.17 Squadron deployed its helicopters in three Flights. 'A' Flight was formed at Swartkop near Pretoria, 'B' Flight at Bloemspruit near Bloemfontein in the Orange Free State and 'C' Flight, (also the training flight with Alouette IIs), at Ysterplaat. In April 1973, the Alouette IIs were withdrawn from use and sold to the Rhodesian Air Force for use on training duties.

More Alouette IIIs were delivered in 1967, to form No.16 Squadron, and later the training Flight was moved to Bloemspruit to become 87 Helicopter Flying School (87 HFS). Further Alouette III deliveries arrived in 1975, some from the United States. These were civil-registered airplanes imported by a private South African company. Fourteen of the twenty-two delivered were taken on SAAF charge.

The last eight of the 118 Alouette IIIs delivered were ex-Rhodesian Air Force/ex-Portuguese Air Force airplanes. It is believed these were attrition replacements for the airplanes lost by the SAAF during missions flown in Rhodesia from 1967 onwards as part of the combined operations to counter the influx of insurgents into that country. SAAF Alouette II and III units were supporting the South African Police (SAP) as they defended the Rhodesian border along the Zambezi River.

By the mid-1970s outside political pressure brought to bear on the RSA had resulted in the progressive withdrawal of the SAP from Rhodesia, but some SAAF Aylos and Cessna C.185 observation planes were still operating clandestinely as part of Operation *Polo*. These airplanes were painted in Rhodesian Air Force (RhAF) camouflage scheme - dark earth/dark green, with no national markings - and the crews wore Rhodesian blue or camouflage uniforms. The highly sensitive nature of South Africa's continued 'Most Secret' involvement in the Rhodesian Bush War demanded that all SAAF airplanes and personnel be 'assimilated' into the RhAF. Communication between the two Air Force headquarters was only allowed at the highest level.

Thirty-five Alouette IIIs remain in use today (2003), on communications, liaison, SAR and rotary-wing training duties. Operated by No.17 Squadron at Swartkop, No.19 Squadron at Louis Trichardt and No.22 Squadron at Ysterplaat, as well as 87 Helicopter Flying School (HFS) at Bloemspruit. Thirty Agusta A109LUH helicopters are on order to replace the Alouette IIIs still in use on utility and support duties. Denel are to build twenty-five of the thirty on order, all to be delivered by 2005, with the first squadron to be operational in 2004.

Agusta A109s are to replace the remaining Alouette IIIs. Planned Initial Operational Capability (IOC) 2004. *(author)*

In 1964, six Westland Wasp HAS 1 helicopters arrived from the UK to be operated by No.22 Flight at Ysterplaat, for use initially aboard two old South African Navy destroyers, SAS *Simon van der Stel* and SAS *Jan van Riebeeck* until embarking the anti-submarine frigates, SAS *President Kruger, President Steyn* and *President Pretorius*. With half of the original deliveries already lost by 1966, an additional four Wasps were ordered and delivered. One of the original Wasps (serial 82), lost off Cape Town was recovered by the sea fisheries vessel *Gamtoos* and over a period of eight years was restored to flying condition. A further seven Wasps were ordered in the early 1970s, but with a change in Government in Britain, only six were delivered. A seventh machine (an army Scout) was obtained from the Bahrain Police. It carried the registration BSP 1 and the letters "GT" on its nose, which it is believed stood for "Gearbox Test". The airplane used for testing Wasp gearboxes. It is of interest this helicopter never carried a SAAF serial and it never flew in South Africa ! The Wasps retired progressively from 1988, and five survivors (2 flyable, 3 as spares) were sold to Singapore in August 1992.

Westland Wasp HAS 1 were among early rotary wing assets (author)

57

In the 1970s, the SAAF became the second biggest operator of the Aerospatiale SA 330 Puma medium lift helicopter after the French Air Force and French Army Aviation (ALAT). The SAAF was the first foreign buyer of the Puma and twenty C models were ordered for delivery in 1970. No.19 Squadron was reformed at Swartkop AFB and was soon split into two Flights with 'A' Flight remaining at Swartkop and 'B' Flight at Durban. Durban was chosen as a Puma base due to the large number of rescue call outs in the frequent bad weather along the coast and to climbing accidents in the nearby Drakensberg Mountain area. B Flight eventually became No.15 Squadron. The unit tasked not only of inland flying beyond the Drakensburg mountains and the coastline from Mozambique down to Lesotho, but also with Army support. SA 330 Pumas were also operated by Nos. 17, 19, 22, and 30 Squadrons at Swartkop, Louis Trichardt and Ysterplaat respectively. No. 30 Squadron disbanded in November, 1991. No.15 Squadron subsequently relinquished its Pumas for nine Eurocopter BK 117A-1/3 deployed on utility and support duties and indigenous Atlas Oryx for army support.

SA 330 Pumas formed the backbone of the rotary-wing fleet throughout the Bush War years. *(author)*

The Pumas of Nos. 15, 22 (and ZS-HJA), and 30 Squadron on 4 August 1991, took part in a massive rescue operation to save all 219 passengers and crew on the stricken cruise liner *Oceanos* which went aground off the South African coast. This difficult but highly successful rescue involved No.30 Squadron alone in more than 78 flying hours. That the details of this dramatic rescue took a back seat in the eyes of the world, was the alarming news , that with the world looking on, the captain of the vessel insisted on being one of the first to be lifted off ! Leaving the rest of the passengers and other crew members aboard the vessel that was in real danger of breaking up. SAAF fixed-wing assets involved in the *Oceanos* rescue was a Transall C-160 and a C-130 Hercules in support of the paramedics.

The ongoing Bush Wars saw the Puma used extensively in South West Africa (Namibia), in support of the ground forces and for casualty evacuation. The type has proved to be one of the most successful and reliable rotary-winged airplanes operated. Further deliveries of the type took place in 1975, with a total of 69 on inventory at one time, including C, H (47) and L (2) variants. The majority of H variants were later converted to L configuration. Two SA 330Js (ZS-HJA and ZS-HIZ) dedicated to the South African Antarctic research facility, were also in the inventory. The types attrition rate was relatively low and of the nine lost most were in front-line combat operations. Subsequently all Puma variants have been withdrawn from use, with around twenty-three believed to be stored at Atlas Aviation, at Jan Smuts.

Sgt J Kruger

Two SA 330J Pumas dedicated to the South African Antarctic research facility, carried an unique colour scheme and civil registrations *(ad astra)*

SAAF heavy-lift helicopter needs were also satisfied by Sud - Aerospatiale by way of 16 Super Frelon SA 321Ls ordered in 1966, and delivered between April 1967 and September 1969. The 321L without floats or radar, was a modified version of the SA 321K non-amphibious transport and assault version developed for Israel. Three Super Frelons were written off in accidents, with one attrition replacement (c/n 185) supplied for SAAF serial 305 (c/n 120) that crashed on 29 September 1971, carrying the same SAAF serial ! The Super Frelon proved to be an excellent workhorse in SAAF service both as a troop transport and in delivery of supplies to remote areas, or on humanitarian missions. The type was finally withdrawn from use at the end of 1990.

SAAF Sud SA 321 Super Frelon helicopters were similar to those delivered to Israel. Example shown is similar Libyan AF model. *(author)*

Sanctions and the need for a Puma and Super Frelon replacement led to the Atlas Aircraft Corporation developing the Puma to a similar standard as the Aerospatiale AS 332 Super Puma to enter SAAF service as the "Oryx". Having initially been given the name Gemsbok. Essentially it was the SA 330 airframe refitted with two uprated engines similar to the twin Makila turboshafts fitted to the Aerospatiale Super Puma and an uprated transmission, desert filters, cockpit displays redesigned for single pilot NVG operation, ventral fin and tailplane of the AS 532 Cougar, plus nose radar. The first Atlas Oryx AS-330S2 Super Puma entered service in 1988, but did not become operational with No.19 Squadron until 1994. With later deliveries equipping No.15 Squadron at Durban in 1996. In 2003, with fifty Atlas Oryx in its battle order it is the SAAF's premier rotary-wing asset.

Development of the prototype CSH-1(Combat Support Helicopter) began in 1985. Originally based on the Aerospatiale AS 330 Puma, the resultant CSH-2 Rooivalk (Red Kestrel) attack helicopter is different in several respects to the Puma; with an entirely new airframe the engines are set well back to facilitate the rear-seated pilots field of vision, while the rear drives from the twin 1580 shp Turbomeca Turmo IVC engines have been taken up through the former tail-rotor drive coupling.

The engine intakes are shielded from dust by adapted Puma particle separator assemblies, whilst the Aerospatiale tricycle landing gear has been replaced by a high-absorption main undercarriage forward and a tail-wheel behind the ventral fin. Self-protection systems such as cooled exhausts, infra-red jammers, flare/chaff dispensers and radar warning system are not fitted as standard equipment. Armament includes locally produced air-to-surface missiles, 68 mm unguided rockets carried in two pods fitted on each of the short stub pylons with V-3 series air-to-air missiles, as carried by the Mirage F.1AZs in Angola fitted at the pylon tips and a turreted under-nose Amscor GA-1 20 mm cannon. The chin-mounted optical turret does not have direct-view optics, although it is stabilised and contains FLIR with automatic tracking. The rear cockpit is fitted with a head-up display to assist the pilot in aiming the unguided rockets. Twelve Rooivalk equip No.16 Squadron at Bloemspruit AFB. Currently these are the air arms newest rotary-wing assets, although four AgustaWestland Super Lynx 300s have been ordered for ASW/ASuW duties. Currently (2003) the only SAAF helicopters with a maritime tasking are the Aerospatiale Alouette IIIs remaining on No.22 Squadrons inventory at Ysterplaat AFB near Cape Town.

Atlas Rooivalk CSH-2 displays
its weapons capability *(author)*

Atlas Aviation Rooivalk company demonstrator (ZU-AHC) in the Bush. *(Photo, Denel/Atlas Aviation)*

Four Westland Super Lynx 300 are order to avail SAAF a shipbourne ASW/ASuW capability in the 21st Century.
(example RDAF) *(author)*

61

5. The 'new' SAAF

The peace agreement over Namibia in 1989, and the Republic of South Africa's emergence from its long period of isolation and sanctions, resulted in the SAAF being greatly scaled-down with less facilities and less airplanes. Its offensive capability was reduced considerably, as the emphasis switched to peacetime support and defence. President de Klerk's bold initiative to abandon apartheid and permit elections for all South Africans gave rise to a massive scaling down and realignment of the SAAF.

In the past, extraordinary circumstances had prevented the SAAF from obtaining its airplanes from the major suppliers in direct sales and at times the air arm was forced to adopt unorthodox measures to meet its requirements. The Atlas Aircraft Corporation became heavily involved in military aircraft design and development, as well as manufacture and maintenance. This permitted the SAAF the ability to ensure it was armed and equipped with the highest standard of equipment to counter those opposing South Africa much of which was the latest types supplied and operated by the Soviets and its communist allies. It is beyond doubt that South Africa's actions in the local guerilla wars helped to arrest the spread of communism in the region.

The SAAF emerged from the Bush Wars, into a peacetime situation with a core of front-line personnel experienced in air warfare, to form the basis of the 'new' air force. Already the air arm was turning its attention to humanitarian operations, its helicopters deployed in flood relief work in SWA and Lesotho and its Hercules transports worked on the multi-national Somali airlift, with supplies being flown into Kenya. Assistance is also provided to neighbouring countries to train, personnel and provide airborne support for local police forces, including drug interdiction, local disturbances, as well as mountain and air-sea-rescue work. Coastal protection duties are also undertaken.

Prior to the UN sanctions, the air force obtained most of its equipment from the UK, Italy and France. Inevitably, the longer the period of isolation went on, many fighter planes and helicopters became outdated and needed replacement. With supplies from the outside world difficult to obtain, the only alternative was for local industry to rebuild existing airframes and to incorporate the latest technical advancements. Amongst the most notable were the conversion of the Dassault Mirage IIIs by Atlas into Cheetahs, the modification of many of the elderly Douglas C-47 Dakota (Skytrain) fleet into Turbo Daks with turboprop engines and construction of the Oryx and Rooivalk helicopters. In the early 1970s Atlas also designed two simplified light planes to perform forward air control (FAC) and transport duties suited for the rugged terrain in southern Africa. This included forty Atlas AM.3C Bosbok, a South African version of the Aermacchi AM.3C, which were sold as part of the rationalisation of the SAAF, at the end of 1992. For a period four Bosboks formed an SAAF aerobatic display team named "Spikes". The other light transport was the Atlas C-4M Kudu produced in 1974 from the Aermacchi AL60, which had already proved its capabilities in the bush with the Rhodesian Air Force since 1967. There was a high commonality of parts between the two types, such as the same engine and wing. The Rhodesian version had a tricycle undercarriage whereas Atlas fitted the Kudu with a tail wheel instead of a nose-wheel. Forty were assembled/manufactured locally by Atlas, the first entering SAAF service in 1974. The survivors finally withdrawn from use and sold off in 1991, to civil operators.

Restructuring of the flying training facilities began in 1993, with the CFS located at the all grass airfield at Dunnottar moving to the southern coastal base of Langebaanweg, the former home of the Impala I jet trainers of 83 Jet Flying School (JFS) and No.7 Squadron, a Citizen Force unit equipped with Impala Is and IIs. Langebaanweg is also home to the SAAF fighter squadrons when using the local weapons firing range. The CFS has responsibility to bring students to 'Wings' status and to stream them for fast jet, transport or helicopter flying. As well as retraining and instructor training and basic courses for neighbouring countries personnel. These duties have remained essentially the same since the introduction of the Pilatus PC 7 'Astra' turbo trainer in 1995, except that some of the Impala training courses were transferred to the CFS syllabus and senior instructors received their training from a Pilatus instructor. The Astra course based upon that conducted by the RAF on its Shorts Tucano primary trainer in the UK, adjusted to meet SAAF requirements. Student pilots will fly in the order of 185 hours in the Astra and some forty hours in the Astra Cockpit Procedural Trainer (CPT) simulator. With a ratio of two students to one instructor most will be ready to fly solo after approximately sixteen hours instruction.

From the CFS, new pilots are transferred to either 85 Advanced Flying School (AFS) at Hoedspruit with Impala I and II for those selected for fast jet flying, 86 Multi-Engine Flying School (MEFTS) with Casa CN.235 and C.212-200 and Douglas C-47TP or 87 Helicopter Flying School (HFS) with Alouette III and Oryx helicopters, both of the latter units based at Bloemspruit. 85 AFS syllabus includes conversion, training in tactical skills, electronic warfare, anti-shipping strike, basic aircraft recognition, military science and meteorology. Including around six to seven months basic jet conversion on the two-seat Impala I. There is also photographic training course which also lasts for six or seven months. In addition the unit undertakes instructor conversion, instrument re-categorisation and tactical training of Cheetah back-seaters (WISOs), Weapons Systems Operators.

The South African coastline stretches well in excess of 1,600 km (1,000 miles) from the Atlantic to the Indian Oceans. These waters are part of the world's major shipping routes and the South African Air Force and Navy are tasked with coastal patrol duties to ensure international and national regulations are adhered to and to carry out numerous maritime search and rescue sorties when needed. Post-war the air force deployed its Short Sunderland flying-boats on these tasks, until their withdrawal in 1955. Subsequently, in August 1957, this became the premise of No.35 Squadron at Cape Town equipped with Avro Shackleton MR.3s. Close-inshore patrols and fishery protection duties were undertaken by No.27 Squadron based at D F Malan/Cape Town IAP, from 1969 until October 1990. Twenty Italian Piaggio P166S were procured, in two batches of ten for this task, the last delivery made in August, 1974. Only one Albatross, as they were known in SAAF service was lost on operations when serial 894 crashed off Dassen Island on 6 May 1976. The reason for the crash remains unknown.

The Avro Shackletons were withdrawn from use on 22 November 1984, mainly due to lack of airframe hours and in order the air force should not lose experienced maritime crews, four Douglas C-47 Dakota Skytrains which had been converted for navigator training were switched to maritime patrol use in January 1985. Ironically, the Dakotas were of a similar age to the Sunderlands the Shackletons had replaced thirty years earlier ! With its crew of seven or eight and a useful six hour duration when on patrol over South Africa's heavily-used coastal waters the Dakotas, designated C-47B-35-DK, were found to be well suited to the task and this gave rise to the upgraded turboprop C-47TP conversion being selected for this task. As well as its primary maritime role No.35 Squadron also undertakes drogue target-towing for the Army, and navigator training. The unit also operates a Beech Super King Air 200C on communications work in and around Cape Town.

Capt J Smith   At one time the Atlas Impala II strike plane equipped all six Tactical Support Command squadrons *(ad astra)*

64

Being virtually self-sufficient No.35 Squadron provides further training for pilots arriving fresh from 86 MEFTS at Bloemspruit including night and formation flying, supply dropping, long-range navigation and low-level flying, including landing on minimally prepared landing surfaces. Frequently, training exercises can take on a more front-line role with the airplanes tasked to drop special buoys into the Atlantic and Indian Oceans for ocean current monitoring and research.

In addition to maritime patrol duties at one time the venerable Dakota formed the backbone of the transport fleet. Flown by No.44 Squadrons 'B' Flight from Swartkop until July 1992, when it moved to Waterkloof along with 'A' Flights small fleet of remaining Douglas C-54s and DC 4s used on a variety of tasks until these were withdrawn from use in 1992, as part of the rationalisation programme. Transferred from South African Airways to the SAAF in 1966, later they were used to great effect transporting troops and supplies to bases in SWA (Namibia) and as airborne command posts and staff transports in Angola.

In 2003, excepting for four C-160 Transalls, general transport duties are the premise of the Lockheed C-130 Hercules, seven of which were acquired for use by No.28 Squadron at Waterkloof in 1963, as Douglas C-47 replacements! No.28 Squadron operates a regular shuttle service for military personnel and light cargo from its home base to all the major base locations in South Africa. It also transports ground crews and equipment on operational exercises and deployments and any police operations requiring air transport support. While No.35 Squadrons Dakletons, have a useful eleven hour duration, long-range overwater search and rescue duties are undertaken in the Hercules in co-operation with the Maritime Rescue Control Centre at Silvermine near Cape Town.

The Hercules were upgraded in the late 1960s, receiving avionics improvements, strengthened wings and the Allison T.56-A-7 engines were retrofitted with the more powerful A-15s. With a strengthened undercarriage and the fitting of a multiple braking system this considerably improved the transports rough field capability. The recent acquisition of five ex-US Navy airplanes has increased the overall operational C-130 Hercules inventory to nine, all of which have received a mid-life upgrade, extending their in-service life by around twenty years . The first three upgrades were completed in the UK at Marshalls of Cambridge, the remainder by Denel in South Africa. Two of the former US Navy airplanes are suffering corrosion problems but may be refurbished for the maritime role. If needed the Hercules fleet can be supplemented by twelve Lockheed L-100-30 Hercules civil aircraft operated by SAFAIR FREIGHTERS.

Previously, American reluctance to sell the Republic of South Africa further C-130 Hercules lead to procurement of the Franco-German Transall C.160 medium tactical transport. Undertaking a wide series of tasks No. 28 Squadron operated the fleet of nine Transall C.160Zs, all of which were received between July 1969 and December, 1970. The type was operated very successfully by the SAAF and was involved in many rescue operations and re-supply operations in South West Africa (Namibia). The Transalls and Hercules were used by South African paratroopers in the their large-scale attacks on SWAPO bases at Cassinga in Southern Angola. No Transall C.160s were lost in flying accidents although the first of two similar incidents involving the type occurred on 31 May 1980, when serial 332 made a wheels-up landing at Mpacha AFB in the Caprivi Strip off SWA (Namibia). The second incident involved serial 339 when the pilot failed to lower the landing gear whilst coming in to land at Waterkloof AFB in the 1980s. SAAF Transalls were retired in January, 1993, and placed in open storage at Waterkloof. Attempts to dispose of them were unsuccessful and one was allocated to the SAAF Museum at Swartkop. Of the remainder, four were reinstated into No. 44 Squadrons inventory in 1996, to permit redeployment of its C-47TPs to other units.

Early operations during the War in Angola conducted from forward operating bases made SAAF senior officers realise what was needed was an air-to-air refuelling capability. Procured during the period of sanctions among those types considered the most suitable choice was the Boeing B.707 as there were numerous surplus airframes available on the second-hand market and countries willing to undertake the conversions. Four B.707-328Cs were bought and No.60 Squadron was reactivated, to operate them, with the arrival of the first three airplanes at Waterkloof AFB in 1986.

They were all converted by IAI of Israel with a three-point hose and drogue system and one had been equipped for the dual-role of tanker and electronic surveillance. For its latter role, an extensive electronic intelligence gathering suite had been installed. Later the other two tankers were also fitted out to the same standard, with the GSY 1501 ELINT/SIGINT gathering system. One aircraft is dedicated for training. Two more B.707-328Cs were obtained in the early 1990s, with one modified with a plush interior and an extensive communications suite for the VIP role, by No. 60 Squadron personnel.

Later, two airplanes underwent further conversion for the AEW role by IAI using the Elton Phalcon System side-fuselage antenna, but not nose and tail radomes. All the airplanes were initially operated in great secrecy without national insignia, although these were subsequently applied to conform to international regulations. The types first public appearance was when serial 1415 was on static display, when Pietersburg AFB had its closing down parade in September, 1992. Previous to this the only indication of their existence to the general public was their regular take-off and landings at Waterkloof. The types first appearance at an air show, was at the Bloemspruit AFB in May 1992, when one airplane made a slow flypast with three Atlas Cheetah Ds in position off the re-fuelling stations.

The southern African terrain, especially in the central and northern regions is largely undeveloped, with few roads and the air force has relied heavily on light planes to perform liaison and observation duties in these remote areas. In the early post-war years the SAAF/SA Army relied on British Auster light AOP planes for observation duties. Initially the SAAF and army evaluated the Dornier Do 27 as a replacement but finally choose the Cessna C.185A Skywagon. The first twenty-four arrived during 1962, and were assigned to No. 42 Squadron at Potchefstroom which at the time was under the control of the army, although the squadron and the airplanes were transferred to air force control in October, 1968. Further Cessnas were delivered, twelve C.185Ds in 1965, four C.185Es in 1967, and the last five C.185Es in 1968.

The Cessnas primary role was observation and aerial reconnaissance, which it performed from a variety of forward operating bases along the border with Mozambique, Rhodesia (Zimbabwe) and Botswana. When deployed 'up country', the squadron had acquired a number of surplus military vehicles for use as mobile accommodation, and to serve as a galley and field maintenance support for the deployed airplanes and personnel. The C.185s versatility, in addition to its more conventional duties, saw it deployed as an airborne command and control post, on aerial pamphlet dropping, message broadcasting (sky-shouting), para-dropping and casualty evacuation.

In 1974, with the entry into service of the Atlas AM.3C Bosbok and C-4M Kudu, the Cessnas were retired from use and placed in storage. However, with both of the Atlas Aviation types withdrawn from use in 1992, the Cessnas were returned to service that year at Swartkop. Three airplanes were flown in a civilian-style red and white colour scheme with civil-registrations until 1996, when they had their military serials applied. They had been used to assist the police patrol built-up areas to track criminals as the Cessnas' colour scheme did not attract undue attention; members of the public and criminals alike paying it little attention as it flew overhead, assuming it was a small civilian plane. Currently nine Cessna C.185s remain in the SAAF's battle order with a secondary role as forward air controllers.

No. 2 Squadrons 'Big Cat' Cheetah C, formates on an unmarked No. 60 Squadron Boeing 707-328 ELINT/SIGINT refueller (*T. Shia*)

For the general utility role, the air force introduced twelve Cessna C.208 Caravan Is, into service assigned to No. 41 Squadron at Waterkloof. The airplanes were delivered between May 1988 and January 1990, to replace the Atlas Bosboks and Kudus. Upon delivery, for six years the Cessnas were operated in civil registrations, with pilots wearing civilian clothes rather than SAAF uniforms, but have since had military serials applied. Although, they still have varying colour schemes and some do not carry flags or SAAF markings. In 2003, eleven Cessna C.208s remain on No. 41 Squadrons inventory along with two Beech Super King Air 200C a King Air 300, and a Pilatus PC 12.

An additional boost to the air arms light plane assets was provided by the 'Air Commando' squadrons. The *'Kommandos'* using civil planes, mainly Cessnas and Pipers, were annotated squadron Nos 101 to 114 (less 113) with 114 an all-female unit. As a part-time 'Volunteer Reservist' operation, it permitted the SAAF to 'borrow' suitable airplanes for specific secondary tasks when and as the need arose from private/owner pilots. In this way those pilots wishing to make an important contribution to SAAF operations, for example to ferry senior service personnel to meetings and operational exercises etc., could do so, while receiving recompense for the use of their time and airplanes.

The proximity of Waterkloof AFB to Johannesburg and Pretoria made it a natural choice for the location of No. 21 (VIP) Squadron. A variety of types are operated to transport senior military personnel and government ministers on business within South Africa as well as to neighbouring countries. At present (2003) the squadron operates two Cessna 550 Citation IIs, one special 'VIP' Douglas C-47TP, one Boeing Biz Jet (BBJ) for long-range duties and two Dassault Falcon 50s. The VIP-configured BBJ and the two Falcon 50s are registered to the Director General of the Department of Transport, for government use, although they are part of No. 21 Squadron. Apart from carrying dark and light blue 'cheatlines', which are the official air force colours, the six airplanes display no traces of military ownership, otherwise appearing in civilian-style livery and with civil (ZS-) registrations.

A single Beech Super King Air 200C is operated in and around Cape Town by No. 35 Squadron on comms duties *(example USAF)* *(author)*

A further civil-register airplane operated by the SAAF for more than thirty years for the South African Government was a lone Vickers Viscount Srs 781D (serial ZS-LPR) delivered in November, 1958.

This airplane was used expressly for the transport of the Governor General of the Union of South Africa and when South Africa became a Republic (RSA) in 1961, it was retained for use by the state President and the name "CASTEEL" was carried on the nose. When not needed for Presidential duties it was used to transport foreign VIPs and dignitaries around South Africa. The air force finally disposed of the airplane to Field Aviation in August 1991, who then resold it to a civil operator in Zaire.

On 10 May 1994, the day on which the South African free elections took place, the SAAF inherited a variety of types from the former small air arms of the independent homelands of Tanskei, Bophuthswana,Venda and Ciskei (TVBC), as when not recognised by the outside world, they were reunified into South Africa. These parts of South Africa had earlier gained independence and established their own small defence forces with a small transport only air facility. Among the types inherited were three Casa 212-200C and one 300 Aviocars, the prototype Airtech CN-235 medium transport, three Pilatus PC 7 (two since retired) subsequently passed on to the CFS at Langebaanweg, and a Pilatus PC 6 Turbo Porter (BopAF serial T-320), subsequently, also retired. A Cessna 551 Citation (VDF-030) of the Venda Defence Force was added to No.21 Squadrons inventory. Nine Eurocopter (MBB) BK.117 helicopters also bolstered the SAAF's rotary-wing assets. The BK 117s remain in use in 2003, with No.15 Squadron at Durban.

Two Pilatus PBN BN 2A Islanders and an Aerospatiale SA.365N1 Dauphin helicopter were taken on charge by the Test & Development Centre at Bredasdorp. This unit otherwise 'borrowing' its air assets as required from the front-line squadrons. Later the SA.365 was transferred to No.17 Squadron at Swartkop.

Two Pilatus PBN BN 2A Islanders are used by the SAAF Test and Development Centre, at Bredasdorp.
(example Pilatus Britten-Norman Bembridge, IoW, UK.)

The following TBVC acquisitions were disposed of:-

Serial	Type	Constructors No.	Origin
T-200	Alouette III	1659	BopAF
T-400	Alouette III	2360	BopAF
VDF-001	Alouette III	2363	Venda Defence Force
ZS-LSN	Cessna C.152	85900	Ciskei Defence Force
ZS-LSP	Cessna C.152	85883	Ciskei Defence Force
ZS-LSA	Piper PA-16 Super Cub	18-7753	Ciskei Defence Force
ZS-KMX	Short Skyvan SC-7	SH-1965	Ciskei Defence Force
ZS-LFG	Short Skyvan SC-7	SH-1977	Ciskei Defence Force

SAAF Battle Order : — Circa December 1995/96

Unit	Equipment	Base
No. 1 Squadron	Mirage F.1AZ	Hoedspruit
No. 2 Squadron	Atlas Cheetah C / D	Louie Trichardt
No. 8 Squadron	Atlas Impala I & II	Bloemspruit
No. 15 Squadron	Atlas Oryx, Eurocopter BK 117	Durban
No. 17 Squadron	Alouette III, Atlas Oryx, SA 365N	Swartkop
No. 19 Squadron	Alouette III, Atlas Oryx	Louis Trichardt
No. 21 (VIP) Squadron	Cessna C 550 Citation, Falcon 50, Falcon 900 HS-125-400B	Waterkloof
No. 22 Squadron	Alouette III, Atlas Oryx, SA330J Puma (2)	Ysterplaat
No. 28 Squadron	Lockheed C-130B	Waterkloof
No. 35 Squadron	C-47TP, Beech King Air 200C (3)	D.F. Malan (Cape Town)
No. 41 Squadron	Cessna C.208 Caravan I	Waterkloof
No. 42 Squadron	Cessna C.185A/D/E, Pilatus PC-6	Swartkop
No. 44 Squadron	C-47TP, C-160 Transall (4) 1996	Waterkloof
No. 60 Squadron	Boeing B.707-328	Waterkloof
Central Flying School (CFS)	Pilatus PC 7 Mk II 'Astra'. North American Harvards - (being withdrawn)	Langebaanweg
85 Combat Flying School (CFS)	Atlas Impala I & II	Hoedspruit
86 Multi-Engined Flying School	C-47TP, Casa 212, CN 235 (1)	Bloemspruit
87 Helicopter Flying School (HFS)	Alouette III, Atlas Oryx	Bloemspruit

Casa C-212 Aviocar light transports are operated by No. 44 Squadron from their base at Waterkloof. *(ad astra)*

75th Anniversary Hercules circa 1995. *(T. Shia)*

6. '75' in Ninety-Five

Having began life on the 1 February 1920, at Zwartkop, near Pretoria, in celebration of being the second oldest air force in the world it was fitting that the 75th anniversary celebrations held at the air arms most inaccessible air base, Hoedspruit in the Eastern Transvaal, saw over 100,000 people attend. Also people attending the Langebaanweg airshow were treated to a rare display of fast jet flying as this base is situated well away from built up areas. As well as a three Cheetah two-on-one dog-fight towards the end of the seven hour flying programme the SAAF staged a first for an air show in South Africa, when two 'fast jets' broke the sound barrier, the first being the SAAF Museum's Dassault Mirage IIICZ serial 800, closely followed by Dassault Mirage F.1AZ serial 226 from No.1 Squadron.

The SAAF has a long and distinguished history, serving alongside the RAF in WW II, participation in the Berlin airlift, and later serving with the UN in Korea. From 1966 to 1989 the SAAF was involved in the Bush Wars in South West Africa (Namibia) and later Angola. In celebration of its 75th Birthday the air arm held an event at each one of its current operational bases. The main 75th Anniversary celebrations were held at Waterkloof AB from 4th-7th October 1995, and were attended by visiting nations from all parts of the world, including Russia.

The first day was mainly a local event with practice flying, followed by a VIP Day on the 5th with the main public display on the remaining two days, when it was estimated over 250,000 people attended. In addition to the SAAF's 75th, the event was an international trade, exhibition and air show with participants from Europe, North America, Australia, the Far East and African nations.

SAAF front-line combat types included No.1 Squadron Mirage F.1AZs serials 225 and 229, with three F.1CZs serials 202, 210 and 211 brought out of store for a hangar photo shoot. No. 2 Squadron provided Cheetah serials 374, 844 and 862. Atlas Impala I trainer serials 522 and 565 came from 85 Combat Flying School (CFS) and an Impala II light ground attack plane was provided by No. 8 Squadron. Transport and force multiplier assets, most of which are resident at Waterkloof were provided by No. 60 Squadron with a Boeing B.707-328 serial AF617, a No. 44 Squadron VIP C-47TP Turbo Dak and a No. 28 Squadron Lockheed C-130B Hercules serial 404 which was displayed resplendent in special 75th Anniversary colour scheme.

No. 41 Squadron displayed one of each type it operated, a Cessna C.208 Caravan I serial 3009 and a Beech King Air 200C serial 651. Three VIP types were on show including the civil-registered HS.125-400B *Mercurius* (ZS-LPF) and Cessna Citation II (ZS-LIG) from No. 21 Squadron and the sole Aerospatiale AS.365 Dauphin VIP helicopter (ZS-HVI) from No.17 Squadron at Swartkop. Adjacent to the transport airplane static display was a recently retired Douglas DC-4 serial 6905.

Training and rotary winged types, as might be expected from the largest operator of the type since WWII, featured the North American T-6 Harvard in a variety of guises including two civil-registered examples (ZU-WLP and ZU-AOR) and four airplanes from the Central Flying School (CFS) at Langebaanweg. This included the personnel mount of the CFS commandant, serial 7001, an airplane rebuilt from the many parts salvaged from others. Serial 7569 was in RAF colours, and serials 7155 and 7156 carried standard CFS livery. Two Swiss Pilatus PC 7 II, T-6 replacements, were displayed in the trade static park, serials 2001 and 2007, while serial 2012 was in the SAAF park. No. 42 Squadron provided two Cessna C.185s, one (serial 748) in the bare metal scheme when the type was used in co-operation with the South African Army and serial 737 in normal SAAF camouflage.

North American Harvard trainers featured prominently in the 75th Birthday celebrations *(T. Shia)*

F/sgt D Rowles

The Harvard Display Team 'ready to go'. *(ad astra)*

Maj A Holtzhausen

The *'Old Growler'* goes vertical. *(ad astra)*

The SAAF displayed four types of helicopters, in addition to the VIP Dauphin, was Alouette III serial 611 in rescue colours, Eurocopter BK 117 serial 388 and two Atlas Oryx serials 1208 and 1232. Atlas Aviation had its Rooivalk attack helicopter demonstrator (ZU-AHC) in the trade hangar. As befitting a 75th Birthday, representative types from the past battle orders were in abundance.

South African Airlines Historic Flight :
Junkers Ju-52   ZS-AFA   (a Casa 352)
Douglas DC 3   ZS-BXF
Douglas DC 4   ZS-BMH
NA Harvard T-6

SAAF Museum Historic Flight : (see appendix)
Avro Shackleton MR 3 serial 1722/P
Fieseler Fi 156 Storch   VD+TD
Piaggio 166S Albatross   serial 881
Douglas C-47 Dakota   serial 6859
Alouette II   serial 22
D.H. Tiger Moth ZS-BXB
Piston Provost   (ex-RhAF)

Historic aircraft operated by 85 Combat Flying School:
Dassault Mirage IIICZ serial 800
D.H Vampire T.55   serial 277
Atlas Impala II 'Gannet' serial 10630

Overseas visitors static display:
Antonov An-124A serial RA 82012
Boeing CC-137   serial 13703 Canadian Armed Forces
Boeing KC-135R   serial 38023 from Mildenhall, UK
Boeing E 3 Sentry serial ZH104 in RAF 80th Anniversary colours.
Dassault Mirage 2000 serial 2-FG *Armée de l' Air*
General Dynamics F-16C Fighting Falcon   serial 91419, tail code SP (Spangdahlem, Germany)
HS Nimrod MR 2 serial XV258
IAI Arava 201   registration 3D-DAC Swaziland Defence Force Air Wing
Lockheed PC-3 Orion serial 222 US Navy
Lockheed PC-3 Orion serial 656 RAAF
Lockheed C-130 Hercules serial M30-10 Malaysian Air Force
Lockheed C-130 Hercules serial 16803 Portuguese Air Force
Lockheed C-130 Hercules serial 48240 tail code RS (Ramstein, Germany)
Lockheed C141B Starlifter serial 40623 from McGuire AFB, USA
Lockheed KC-10A serial 60035 from McGuire AFB, USA
MDC F-15 Eagle serial 90248 tail code LN (Lakenheath, UK)
Mikoyan MiG-29SM Fulcrum
Red Arrows 'spare' BAe Hawk T1
Transall C-160 serial 64-GY *Armée de l' Air*
Sukhoi Su 27 Flanker

The flying display at Waterkloof was split into two halves. The show was opened by a former Bophutatswana Air Force Pilatus PC 6 Turbo Porter trailing a 'Congratulations SAAF 75' banner; next came Oryx, Alouette III, and Rooivalk helicopters trailing country and air force flags with the SAAF Anniversary C-130 Hercules bringing up the rear.

Atlas Oryx trails the flag. *(ad astra)*

The display proper began with the Atlas Impalas of the *Silver Falcons Display Team* from 85 Combat Flying School with a 15-minute display consisting of formation aerobatics plus a solo flyer. This was followed by a stunning display by a Lockheed Martin company F-16 display pilot in an airplane borrowed from the USAF contingent from Spangdahlem USAF base in Germany. The largest airplane in this segment of the display was a KLM Boeing B.747 'Jumbo Jet', en-route to Johannesburg, which carried out a fly-by. The F-16 Falcon display was followed by a SAAF Oryx helicopter demonstration of agility followed by a Soviet Mikoyan MiG-29 Fulcrum fighter. The Spanish Air Force displayed a Casa CN 235 (serial 35-29) medium transport plane of which one is operated by the SAAF. A light Spanish transport Casa C 212 Aviocar also in the SAAF battle order was used for the *Golden Eagles* parachute team to jump from.

These displays were followed by a display from the oldest type still in SAAF service at the time, the NA Harvard trainer, by way of a brilliant four ship display of close formation aerobatics by the 'old growlers'. As a final salute during the VIP display they performed a complete rolling loop for the first and only time in public. The Harvard Display Team was formed in 1949 and was disbanded in 1965, when the Silver Falcons jets took centre stage, but were reactivated in 1986, to continue to impress the South African public ever since. The Harvards were followed by its successor, the turboprop Pilatus PC 7 'Astra Team', flown by six CFS instructor pilots. The embryo team demonstrating the versatility of the CFS new basic trainer. Twenty Harvards flew in '75' formation over Waterkloof.

These rather sedate airplanes were soon to be upstaged by an 'Super' Mirage F.1CZ fitted with a Soviet Klimov RD-33 engine as used in the Mikoyan MiG-29. One other SAAF F.1CZ is fitted with this powerplant for evaluation, with a view to re-engining eleven stored F.1CZs to return them to front-line service. To continue the fast jet displays the Soviets demonstrated their Sukhoi Su 35 Flanker 'Snakebites' and 'Cobras', that have become a regular feature of international air shows around the world. The overall 'agility' theme continued, with the SAAF's Impala II 'Gannet' put through its paces until the tempo was slowed with the Maritime Turbo Daks, demonstration of what turbo-power had done for it. The Dak pilot lifting its tail off the ground until the fuselage was parallel with the runway before taking off, to carry out a 'Sarajevo', climb out to further demonstrate the greatly improved performance over its WW II C-47 Dakota piston-engined counterpart. The final act of the morning was the RAF's Red Arrows, that brought the huge crowd to a standstill with its breathtaking aerobatics. Most not being aware that the BAe Hawk T.1 trainers flown had not been designed to perform intricate aerobatic manoeuvres in temperatures approaching 32° C at 5,000 feet above sea-level.

The world renouned RAF Red Arrows closed the morning and afternoon sessions of the 75th Anniversary flying display each day at Waterkloof AB. *(T. Shia)*

Atlas assembled Pilatus PC 7 II 'Astra' now fully equip the Central Flying School (CFS) at Langebaanweg. *(T. Shia)*

The afternoon display began with the SAAF Lockheed C-130 Hercules, and Casa C 212 Aviocar light transport displays followed by a solo demonstration by the CFS 'Astra'. Fast jets returned to the flight- line by way of the SAAF's Mirage F.1AZ, the Air Force Museum Historic Flights airworthy Mirage IIICZ and its vintage D. H. Vampire T.55 (serial 277) performing opposition flying with the Impala II 'Gannet'. The Avro Shackleton MR 3 did not become airborne but did carry out a fast run down the runway. The SAAF then launched its Boeing B.707 tanker followed by three Cheetahs including serial 42 in its special 'big cat' markings. The airplanes returned in formation with the Boeing tanker trailing its three-point refuelling hoses, for the Cheetahs to formate on to, after which they performed an airfield attack. After the Cheetahs had landed the Boeing B.707-328 made a series of flypasts to demonstrate what that airplane was capable of.

Following repeat performances by the F-16, MiG-29, Su-35 and Mirage 2000, the BAe Hawk 100 demonstrator serial ZJ100 (in SAAF markings) gave a demonstration of its capabilities followed by the Red Arrows T.1s to close the show. Or so it was thought, but for those who had stayed to the very end on Friday, a previously unannounced flypast was made by an old adversary until 1989, by a Namibian (SWA) Douglas DC 6, that closed the proceedings that day.

No. 60 Squadron Boeing 707-328 dispensing fuel to No. 2 Squadron Cheetah C multi-role combat planes. *(T. Shia)*

Sgt T Kruger

SAAF Museum D.H. Vampire T.55/2 'airs' its wings. *(ad astra)*

Single-seat Atlas Impala 'Gannet' in special CFS 25th Anniversary colours which it kept ever since *(ad astra)*

Sgt W Stolz

Five years later the SAAF's 80th Anniversary was marked at official level by the deployment of three Belgian Air Force F-16s to Africa for the first time, along with seventy-five personnel to participate in Africa Aerospace and Defence 2000 exhibition and airshow at Waterkloof AB, south of Johannesburg. Three Belgian Lockheed C-130 Hercules, a military Airbus and a USAF KC-135 Stratotanker supported the deployment named Operation *Noordvalk*. The only previous deployment of Belgium Air Force fighter planes to South Africa was in July 1959, when four Canadian-built CF-100 Canucks were sent to the Belgian Congo, at the time still a Belgian colony. The official reason given for the deployment was to display the airplanes at an airshow to mark the 10th Anniversary of Kamina Air Base, in Shaba. Although, with the country pushing for independence at the time, it was thought the real purpose was to demonstrate to the local population that Belgium could deploy 'modern' combat planes to the region if needed. Although when trouble arose following the granting of independence the following year on 30 June, only armed Harvard trainers and brand new Fouga Magisters already based at Kamina were involved in the counter-insurgency operations. The only other out of Europe deployments for the Force Aérienne Belge (FAB) has been regular visits to Morocco with its F-16s for two weeks of very Low-Level Flying (VLLF) at Meknès.

The F-16 deployment to South Africa from Europe took place between 28 and 30 August 2000, via Portugal, the Canary Islands, and Libreville (Gabon). The longest leg of the flight was over international waters from Libreville to Waterkloof, the three F-16 fighters and their USAF tanker covering 5,400 km (3,100 nautical miles) in 6.5 hours, with six in-flight refuellings. The return flight to Europe on 18-20 September, followed the same route except for a stop in Dakar (Senegal). While in the RSA one of the FAB pilots, Commander Danny 'Ket' Meersman, won the Denel Trophy for the best international solo aerobatic performance for his display at Waterkloof AFB. On the 31 August, three jets accompanied by a C-130 Hercules transport made a flypast above Cape Town and Robben Island, where ex-President Nelson Mandela was imprisoned during the era of apartheid.

Force Aérienne Belge (FAB) F-16A Fighting Falcon in that air arms anniversary colours. Note: FAB is no longer, now is Army Air Component or COMOPAIR (Command Operations Air) since 2 January 2002. *(author)*

After the flypast, the four airplanes flew on to Louis Trichardt AFB, where in one week between 11 and 15 September, they flew twenty-seven sorties (out of 30 planned), with the Atlas Cheetahs of No.2 Squadron. Some sorties were flown alongside the SAAF interceptor, which also acted as adversaries to the FAB fighters on occasions. The Belgian pilots were impressed by their SAAF counterparts extremely high standard of combat flying, commenting that many of 'the procedures' were similar to those used by the NATO air forces. In spite of a degree of local controversy which surrounded the deployment in a repeat of the CF-100 Chanucks visit forty years earlier, the Belgian Defence Minister, André Flahaut, gave his assurances there were no 'hidden agenda', and the sole object of the visit was to test the FABs long-range deployment capabilities, as requested by the new NATO and EU strategies. Also that he had agreed to the exercise on his visit to South Africa with a view to establishing closer co-operation between the two countries.

7. Very Important Base's

South Africa's most modern and important air base is situated approximately 400 km north of Pretoria at the foot of the Soutpansberg mountain range in the Northern Transvaal. Construction of the base began in 1984 and three years later on 14 October 1987, Louis Trichardt was officially opened by the then Minister of Defence General M. A. Malan.

The base has one runway which is about 5,000 metres long, which enables the resident Cheetah airplanes to operate with a full weapons load even on the hottest of summer days. In addition to the single runway, there is a taxi-way which is wide enough to act as an emergency runway. Like most modern combat airfields, all the No. 2 Squadrons front-line Cheetahs are housed in hardened shelters from which all operations are conducted, including refuelling and arming of the airplanes. The units training flight equipped with combat-capable Cheetah Ds now operate from non-hardened shelters, having originally operated from a conventional flight-line. No.19 Squadrons Alouette IIIs and Oryx helicopters are housed in semi-hardened shelters. Besides providing the airplanes with protection against possible attack, of equal importance is the protection afforded the airplanes and crews from the intense summer sun and very high temperatures.

Disbanded on 2 October 1992, the first operational squadron to operate from Louis Trichardt on 25 March 1988, was No. 5 Squadron, equipped with Atlas Cheetah Es. An interim development of the Dassault Mirage IIIEZ these airplanes were withdrawn from use and placed in storage when the more sophisticated Cheetah C equipped No. 2 Squadron on 26 February, 1993. In 1963, No.2 Squadron had become the first unit in the SAAF's battle order to receive the delta-winged Mach 2 Mirage III. Successively operating the Mirage IIIBZ, and IIICZ single and dual-seat fighters and later the IIIRZ reconnaissance variant, initially from Waterkloof and then at Hoedspruit from 1963, until the type was withdrawn from use and the squadron disbanded in October, 1990.

No.2 Squadron named 'The Flying Cheetahs', after its squadron badge depicting a flying Cheetah, was re-activated at Louis Trichardt in February 1993, to operate the multi-role Cheetah C developed by the Atlas Aircraft Corporation. The last of thirty-eight Cheetah C's ordered were delivered to the squadron in June 1995. At this time a No.2 Squadron Cheetah pilot was normally flying two sorties a day averaging around 250 flying hours a year. More than his NATO counterpart. All maintenance except major servicing is carried out by the squadron with the type returning a good serviceability level.

No. 2 Squadron Cheetah C on dispersal at Louis Trichardt AB *(ad astra)*

Powered by a single SNECMA Atar 9K-50 turbojet engine, the Cheetah C can attain Mach 2 at 11,000 metres altitude and has a range of 300 unrefuelled nautical miles, with a maximum payload of 5,600 kg. It is a multi-role airplane and can operate in the air-to-air, air-to-ground and air-to-sea roles in all weathers and at night. Every Cheetah pilot is trained to fulfil each of these roles, as well as air-to-air refuelling with the Boeing B.707 tankers of No.60 Squadron which form an important part of the Cheetah's mission profile. In the air-to-air role the airplane is equipped with short-range infra-red missiles in addition to its twin DEFA 552A 30mm cannons. When used in the air-to-ground role it can carry up to ten 250-kg (500 lb) Mk.82 bombs or a mixed load of bombs and missiles for self defence. It can also be equipped with 'smart' weapons.

In 1992, with the closure of Pietersburg AFB, the dual-seat Cheetah Ds of 89 Combat Flying School were transferred to No.2 Squadron Training Flight at Louis Trichardt. The training flight operates completely independent from No.2 Squadron and provides operational training for pilots destined to fly the single-seat Cheetah C or the single-seat Mirage F.1AZ operated by No.1 Squadron at Hoedspruit.

Students joining No.2 Squadron Training Flight from 85 AFS, for conversion to Cheetah C first undergo five weeks at the ground school which includes intensive use of the flight simulator. The student pilot then spends the next six months flying 95 hours on the dual-seat Cheetah D and a further 75 hours on the single-seat Cheetah C before qualifying as a fully operational combat pilot. During the conversion course the student pilot would have received instruction in every aspect of modern combat fast jet flying including in-flight refuelling, air-to-air combat (dog-fighting) and air-to-ground attack with live weapons.

On the 10 January 1991, the Cheetahs of No.2 Squadron were joined by No.19 Squadron 'E' Flight at its new base, operating Aerospatiale Alouette III and Atlas Oryx helicopters. The unit redesignated No.19 Squadron in 1992. The Oryx is a local Atlas Aviation highly advanced development of the SA330 Puma easily distinguished from its predecessor by its nose radar thimble. Powered by two Topaz engines a locally-developed version of the Aerospatiale SA 332 Super Puma's Turbomeca Makilas. The fact the Oryx weighs approximately the same as the Puma from which it was derived, it returns a very impressive performance. The Soutpansberg mountain range provides No.19 Squadrons pilots and crew with the opportunity to train in varied conditions with the Oryx's very modern avionics fit, including a Global Positioning Satellite (GPS) system, weather radar, and mapping facility.

No.19 Squadron's Oryx are used for rapid reaction force deployments in addition to their normal medium and heavy lift transport duties. Mountain SAR and fire-fighting operations using the 'Bambi' bucket also form an important part of the Oryx's deployments. The Oryx also has the ability to operate at night with the aid of Night Vision Goggles (NVG). The squadrons Alouette IIIs are now mainly used for general communication duties, although they still provide back-up for mountain search and rescue (SAR). They also provide support for the South African Police Air Wing especially in marijuana crop destruction operations.

Since the beginning of the 1990s, more than half of the SAAF's front-line types have been withdrawn and six of its bases and air stations have closed. Of those that remain, Hoedspruit sited in the Eastern Transvaal lowveld, 440 km from Pretoria, is less than 150 km from the Mozambique border. Today, Hoedspruit AFB remains one of the SAAF's important bases, as it is home to all twenty Mirage F.1AZ fighter ground attack planes of No.1 Squadron. Hoedspruit together with Louis Trichardt housing the Cheetah fleet, are the last SAAF facilities to house supersonic combat planes.

No. 1 Squadron Mirage F.1AZ equipped with Armscor V3 Kikri heat-seeking AAM lands at Hoedspruit streaming its brake-chute. *(ad astra)*

Hoedspruit AFB was commissioned on 1 July 1978, by the then Defence Minister P. W. Botha, who later became Prime Minister. The bases location underlines its strategic importance in the 'new' SAAF.

The site had been carefully chosen, in the Bush War era, with the design specifically tailored for operational combat planes. Everything on the base is camouflaged, with the most easily recognisable feature, the 4,000 metre runway. It is one of the longest in South Africa and permits the Mirage F.1AZ to take-off fully laden even in the hottest of summer days. The wide taxiways were designed to double as emergency runways. All the base infrastructure was constructed with heavy reinforcement enabling it to withstand all but a direct hit. Many of the important buildings, such as squadron headquarters, have been built underground with access gained through heavy metal doors. The domestic area and crew quarters are located 12 km to the west at Drakensig, which reduces the risk of collateral damage and the loss of valuable trained personnel should the air base come under attack. The air base itself is very large and is located in the middle of a wilderness, close to the Kruger National Park, which itself affords the base a degree of self protection !

In addition to No.1 'Prima' Squadron, Hoedspruit is home to 85 Advanced (Combat) Flying School. No.1 Squadron is the oldest unit in the SAAF battle order, dating back to the formation of the air arm itself. On 1 February 1920 No.1 Flight was officially established at the historic air station at Swartkop. No. 1 Squadron was very effective in WW II emerging with 165 confirmed air-to-air combat "kills" together with 26 probables. Post-WW II the squadron received the de Havilland Vampire FB.5 fighter-bomber as the first jet-powered combat type to operate in South Africa. Earlier twenty loaned USAF North American F-86F Sabres were flown in Korea, by No.2 Squadron (SAAF) but did not operate in South Africa. No.1 Squadron later flew the Canadair F-86 variant, the CL 13B Sabre Mk 6 which was operated until 1975, when the unit disbanded. However, on reformation the squadron operated the Mirage F.1AZ, which it flew to good effect in the Angolan operations.

A total of thirty-two Mirage F.1AZs were ordered from Dassault in July 1971, the prototype making its debut at the Paris Air Show at Le Bourget, in 1975. The F.1AZ was based on the F.1C version (also operated by the SAAF) but differed from the French airplane in that it did not carry the expensive and complex multi-mode Cyrano IV radar which was exchanged for the Aïda II ranging radar optimised for ground attack. The latter equipment considered as ideal to allow ranging for the two DEFA 553 30mm cannons and for guidance of its wing-tip mounted short-range air-to-air missiles during close-in dog-fighting. The airplanes were fitted with an inflight refuelling probe installed high-up forward of the cockpit, adjacent with the types long pointed nose. The SAAF F.1AZs being the first Mirage F.1 variant to be fitted with an air-to-air refuelling capability, many years before the *Armée de l' Air* airplanes. No.60 Squadrons Boeing B.707 inflight refuelling tankers are regular co-inhabitants at Hoedspruit. Luckily, the thirty-two Mirage F.1AZs allocated in the serial range 216 to 247 were delivered between October 1975 and October 1976, before the arms embargo was declared against South Africa on 8 November, 1977.

FAPA MiG-21 and MiG-23 encounters over Angola forced the introduction of a low-viz colour scheme in the 1980s. *(ad astra)*

Since the withdrawal of No. 3 Squadrons F.1CZ, No.1 Squadron is dual-roled, the primary duty of the squadron is ground-attack, with other missions including close air support and deep penetration strike. The airplane is equipped with 125 kg and 250 kg fragmentation bombs or the locally produced 'smart' weapons. Rockets are used only occasionally as their delivery profile is considered highly dangerous for the launch airplane in a high threat environment. No.1 Squadron also performs daytime air defence as a secondary duty. Although not equipped with a dedicated airborne intercept (A.I.) radar, having evolved from the earlier F.1C all-weather interceptor, the F.1AZ possesses good air superiority capabilities, and the squadron's airplanes are now equipped with the latest generation of indigenous short-range infra-red missiles known as V3C Darter, which is highly rated by SAAF pilots as being the best in the world. The Mirage F.1AZs also perform limited reconnaissance missions on occasions, the pilots preferring to use the Mk 1 'Eyeball' to conduct armed visual recce rather than sophisticated photographic equipment.

Having already operated the type for almost thirty years, with the host of local improvements made to its ECM fit and the compatibility with the new 'smart' weapons, No.1 Squadron appears set to continue in its present role for at least another decade, until the introduction of the Saab JAS39 Gripen into SAAF service, in 2009. The squadron was very active during the war in Angola following the types introduction into service in April 1975, although its exact role still remains a closely guarded secret. Indeed, it was not until nineteen months later, that the SAAF publicly acknowledged it was operating the type.

During Operation *Moduler* and Operation *Hooper*, which took place between September 1987 and March 1988, the squadron flew 638 combat missions with the loss of two airplanes. The first loss was to a Surface-to-Air Missile (SAM) while the second was believed to have been due to ground fire during a low-level night mission. At this time with the Soviets making regular deliveries of SAM systems and anti-aircraft batteries into the area the Mirage pilots were confronted with the short-range SA-7 and SA-14s, as well as the deadly longer-range SA-2 ' Grail' and SA-8. Hundreds of missiles were fired at the Mirage F.1s which were forced to operate routinely at tree-top level, in the hope the SAMs would pass harmlessly by them !

To afford a degree of protection against the barrage of ground-based artillery and SAMs the Mirages were fitted with a range of locally developed ECM systems, a RWR (Radar Warning Receiver), as well as chaff dispensers. Other locally developed installations included the fitment of underwing pylons called "station zero' which were dedicated to the ECM system, which increased the airplanes maximum take-off weight by 8%. It is of interest these improvements were subsequently fitted to the French *Armée de l' Air* Mirage F.1CT variants. Early in 1988, the SAAF Mirages were equipped with a defensive chaff dispenser fitted at the vertical tail. This was at the request of the pilots who by this time considered the fitment a necessity whilst they were still required to fly missions into the extremely hostile SAM environment in Angola. Operations over Angola also led to the adoption of a new special low-viz camouflage colour scheme for SAAF combat planes.

Hoedspruit AB also houses 85 Advanced (Combat) Flying School which undertakes conversion and advanced flying training for all pilots destined to fly the Mirage F.1s with the co-located No.1 Squadron or the Cheetahs with No.2 Squadron at Louis Trichardt. 85 AFS is a relative newcomer to Hoedspruit, having moved from Pietersburg on 1 January, 1993. The training units origins lie with the Air Operational School originally based at Langebaanweg. In October 1967, on relocating to Pietersburg the unit became the Advanced Flying School (AFS). The designation 85 Combat Flying School (CFS) adopted in 1982. Initially the AFS was equipped with de Havilland Vampire T.55s until these were replaced by the Atlas Impala I in 1970. The dual-seat Dassault Mirage III was assigned in 1974, along with a number of Canadair Sabres transferred from No.1 Squadron in 1975. Although, the latter was only operated briefly as they were withdrawn from use in 1978. On 1 July 1986, 89 Combat Flying School was established and equipped with the Mirage III, while 85 CFS continued with the dual-seat Impala I for basic combat flying training and it assumed a secondary operational ground-attack role with its single-seat Impala II. In 1995, around sixty Impalas were operated by 85 CFS and included the SAAF's 'Silver Falcons' aerobatic team.

Currently (2003), 85 AFS operates around 48 Impala (30 Is and 18 IIs). It is of interest, 85 CFS celebrated its 25th Birthday in September 1992, and Impala II serial 1063 was given a special colour scheme. Known as 'Gannet' it is believed this airplane has continued to sport this livery ever since and is shown off regularly at air shows and other events in South Africa.

The superb Silver Falcons Atlas Impala I airplanes were distinctly numbered in large numeral '1 to 6' on the tail. *(T. Shia)*

8. South African Police Air Wing

The SAAF's heavy involvement in the Bush Wars, ever rising crime and politically motivated violence led to the formation of a Police Air Wing in 1985, and by 1986, a number of SAAF Alouette IIIs were in operation. Later, these were returned to the air force and the Police Air Wing purchased more up-to-date MBB BK 117 (2), MBB BO105CBS (15) and two Hughes 369Ds. Fixed-wing assets included a Cessna C.402A procured in May 1978, an ex-SAAF Beech Super King Air obtained in September 1983 and eight Pilatus PC-6 Turbo Porters delivered in 1993.

Of these in 2003, only the fifteen MBB BO105 helicopters and eight PC-6 fixed-wing airplanes remain. The BO105s selected for their hot-and-high performance. Each helicopter is fitted with a front bracket mounted SX-16 Nightsun and a locally made forward looking infra-red (FLIR) unit. The Nightsun high-intensity light and FLIR are slaved together so that they continually point in the same direction. The bracket mounts allows for the SX-16 Nightsun to be removed from the helicopter during the day to protect them from the extreme heat, with temperatures in Johannesburg climbing to 40°C.

The SAP Air Wing personnel complement of around 100 includes 36 pilots and maintenance staff most ex-SAAF personnel. The unit has an operational area covering more than 1,219,796 km2. (471,000 sq miles) and provides a service for a population of some 30 million people. It has bases in Pretoria, Johannesburg, Bloemfontein, Port Elizabeth, Cape Town, Durban, Pietersburg, Potchefstroom, Kimberley, Nelspruit. The headquarters located in Pretoria, allocates the air assets on a request basis. Air support, when called up can usually be provided within three to four minutes during daylight hours - and even quicker if the airplane is already in the air on crime prevention control. In a city the size of Johannesburg stretching 80km (50 miles) from east to west and 160km (100 miles) north to south, the response time is truly outstanding. Especially if it is considered this sector has some of the most densely populated areas.

In addition to such tasks as crime prevention (aerial patrol), crowd control, marijuana crop eradication, cattle rustling, motor vehicle theft and photo-reconnaissance, the BO105 is the favoured mount of the armed response (SWAT) teams. Following an incident involving a SWAT team in 1993, a '105' was hit by ground fire while operating as an airborne command post for riot police. As a result locally produced 1.5 in thick armoured-plated seats for the pilot and observer were fitted to all SAP helicopters. Although there has been small number of occasions when the SWAT teams have fired to the ground from the over flying helicopters this is not normal practice and not encouraged by higher authority. For low-level operations such as crowd and riot control, the '105' can fly as low as 60-90 metres (200-300 ft) while still moving at sufficient speed to minimise its target potential.

The MBB BO105CBS is the chosen mount of the SAP Air Wing *(T. Shia)*

Two more powerful MBB BK 117s used mostly for communication flights and some patrol missions, no longer appear on inventory with one, serial ZS-HSE written off on 9 February, 1991. The two Hughes 369D used on a variety of tasks such as *Dagga* (marijuana eradication), the spraying of herbicides, and counter cattle rustling in outlying areas on the border with Mozambique, have also been withdrawn from use.

One of the SAPs MBB BK 117s (ZUS-HSE) was written-off on 9 February 1991. *(author)*

Although the pilots prefer the BO105s, the fixed wing Pilatus PC-6 Porters are valued for their loitering capability at slow speeds and their ability to take off and land (STOL) from roads as well as short strips and runways. Some Porters are based at Rand Airport from where they are used for prolonged low-speed surveillance. Initially the Porters were used as a public relations tool by the SAP to placate the public as they were slow to accept the need for helicopters as part of the Air Wings inventory. Each year the need and expenditure on the Police Air Wings assets are re-assessed and finance is made available based on the number of operational missions flow and any cost savings to the community that may have resulted from the Air Wings intervention on any particular flight.

As the Air Wing operates under strict financial control, it does not carry out its own rotary-wing *ab initio* training of new pilots and such applicants, if not service trained are required to have a commercial licence and a minimum of 800 hours for fixed wing operations or 1,000 hours for helicopters. Many of the Air Wings pilots are dual rated and can fly both types. Since its creation the Air Wing has carried out a number of operations in neighouring Swaziland and has been approached to provide assistance by other neighbours.

South African Police (SAP) Air Wing Equipment (*Past and circa 2002)

Registration	Type	Registration	Type	Registration	Type
ZS-KEG	Cessna C.402A *	ZS-HNY	MBB BO105CBS	ZS-HUZ	MBB BO105CBS
ZS-LNV	Beech Super King Air (Ex-SAAF) *	ZS-HNX	MBB BO105CBS	ZS-RBA	MBB BO105CBS
ZS-MHN	Beech 400 *	ZS-HNW	MBB BO105CBS	ZS-RBB	MBB BO105CBS
		ZS-HNZ	MBB BO105CBS		
ZS-MSZ	Pilatus PC 6	ZS-HRF	MBB BO105CBS	ZS-HSD	MBB BK 117 *
ZS-NIR	Pilatus PC 6	ZS-HRG	MBB BO105CBS	ZS-HSE	MBB BK 117 *
ZS-NIS	Pilatus PC 6	ZS-HRH	MBB BO105CBS	ZS-HWX	Hughes 369D *
ZS-NIT	Pilatus PC 6	ZS-HRI	MBB BO105CBS	ZS-HWY	Hughes 369D *
ZS-NIU	Pilatus PC 6	ZS-HSF	MBB BO105CBS		
ZS-NIV	Pilatus PC 6	ZS-HSG	MBB BO105CBS		
ZS-NIW	Pilatus PC 6	ZS-HUX			
ZS-NIX	Pilatus PC 6	ZS-HUY			

APPENDIX I: South African Air Force (SAAF) Equipment Circa 2003/4

H.Q. Nedbank Centre, Cnr Church and Schubart, Private Bag, X199 0001. Pretoria.

Estimated 85 combat aircraft : 8 attack and several extempore armed helicopters

Interception/Attack
SAAB JAS39 Gripen (Tranche 2/3 standard) (19) On order   *Plus 9 - combat-capable two-seat aircraft. Delivery 2007-12.*
Dassault Mirage IIIEZ Cheetah E2 (13) WFU   *For Sale*

Dassault Mirage F.1CZ (11) WFU   *Two F.1CZ aircraft are used for test purposes.*

Air Superiority
Atlas/IAI Cheetah C/TC2 (28)

Attack
Dassault Mirage F.1AZ (20)   *Fighter Ground Attack*
Atlas Impala II (17)
Atlas Gemisbok AS.532 Super Puma (3)
Atlas CSH-2 Rooivalk (8)
Two modified to Block 1E standard with Mokipa anti-armour missiles and Mistral air-to-air missiles

Recce
Dassault Mirage Cheetah R (1)

Maritime Patrol/PR/EW Training
Douglas C-47TP Dakota (Dakleton) (7)   *(5 maritime patrol, 1 photo-recce duties, 1 EW training)*

Observation/Liaison.
Cessna 185A/D/E (9)   *Forward Air Control*
Cessna Model 208 Caravan 1 (11)
HB-23/2400 Scanliner (12)

A.E.W
Boeing 707-328C (2)

Tanking/ELINT/SIGINT Gathering
Boeing 707-328C (3)   *(1 aircraft for training)*

V.I.P Transport (For Government Use)
Dassault Falcon 50 (2)
Boeing Biz Jet (1)   *VIP transport. Received 2001 to replace Falcon 900*

Transport
Aerospatiale SA 330H/L Puma (23) WFU   *Stored - Atlas at Jan Smuts.*
Atlas Oryx AS-330S2 Super Puma (44)
Beech Super King Air 200C/300 (3/1)
Douglas C-47TP Dakota (4)
Lockheed C-130B Hercules (9)   *Updated, with re-configured cockpit and Thales avionics*
Lockheed L-100-30 Hercules (12)   *Civil aircraft. Operated by "SAFAIR FREIGHTERS"*
*Lockheed C-130E Hercules (3)
*ex-USN * (2 corroded, but could be refurbished for maritime role). Airplanes with No.35 Sqdn at DF Malan, Cape Town*
Note: Updated Hercules life-extended by around twenty years.

Casa 212-100/200 Aviocar (2/2)
Casa CN235 (1)

A single IAe/Casa CN 235 medium transport is operated by No. 44 Squadron at Waterkloof AB. *(author)*

ASW/ASuW
AgustaWestland Super Lynx 300   (4) Ordered   *Confirmed/Signed August 2003*

VIP TRANSPORT
Cessna 550 Citation II   (2)
Pilatus PC-12   (1)   *Comms*

Comms/liaison/SAR
Aerospatiale SA 316B/SA319 Alouette III   (24)   *Training*

Utility/Support
Agusta A109LUH   (30) Ordered   *To replace Alouette IIIs. Option for 10. April 2002-5*
The first A109M squadron to be operational 2004. First deliveries 2003. Denel to build 25 of the 30 ordered.
Eurocopter BK 117A-1/3 (9)

Training
Atlas Impala I   (21)
Cheetah D   (10)   *Combat-Capable (to be replaced by BAe Hawk Mk 120*
C-47TP Dakota   *(in previous total)*
Aerospatiale SA 316B Alouette III   *See Comms/liaison*
Pilatus PC-7 MK II 'Astra'   (53)   *(Also used by Silver Falcons Display Team) Reducing to 40.*
BAe Hawk 120 (24) Ordered.   *Combat-Capable advanced trainer delivery 2005-2009*
 * *Hawk Mk 120. One UK-built airplane first flight March 2003, for delivery to Atlas in South Africa.*
  Atlas deliveries to commence 2005 with first batch of nine, then continuing production of remaining fourteen aiplanes by 2009.

NOTE:-
1. Atlas Impala 1. & II are to be partly replaced, by BAe Hawk Mk 120 with an uprated R-R Adour 951 engine
 * *Hawk is subject of off-set for local manufacture under licence by ATLAS AIRCRAFT. Impala fleet to be reduced to*
  24 aircraft. Hawks will be based at Louis Trichadt AFB in a single squadron, replacing Cheetahs.

South African Police Air Wing
Equipment:
MBB BO105   (15)
Pilatus PC-6 Turbo Porter   (8)

An No. 28 Squadron Lockheed C-130B Hercules receives attention to one of its Allison A-7 turboprop engines on dispersal at Waterkloof AB. *(T. Shia)*

APPENDIX II: SAAF Battle Order — Circa 2003

Unit	Equipment	Base
No. 1 Squadron	Mirage F.1AZ	Hoedspruit
No. 2 Squadron	Atlas Cheetah C / D	Louis Trichardt
No. 8 Squadron	Atlas Impala II	Bloemspruit
No. 15 Squadron	Atlas Oryx, Eurocopter BK 117	Durban
No. 16 Squadron	Atlas Rooivalk CSH-2	Bloemspruit
No. 17 Squadron	Alouette III, Atlas Oryx, SA.365N	Swartkop
No. 19 Squadron	Alouette III, Atlas Oryx	Louis Trichardt
No. 21 (VIP) Squadron	Falcon 50, Boeing Biz Jet, Cessna 550	Waterkloof
No. 22 Squadron	Alouette III, Atlas Oryx, SA 330J (2)	Ysterplaat
No. 28 Squadron	C-130B Hercules, C-130E (1)	Waterkloof
No. 35 Squadron	C-47TP (8), King Air 200C (1)	D.F. Malan (Cape Town)
No. 41 Squadron	Cessna C.208 Caravan I, Super King Air 200C (2) Super King Air 300 (1), Pilatus PC 12 (1)	Waterkloof
No. 44 Squadron	Casa 212, CN235 (1), C-160 (4)	Waterkloof
No. 60 Squadron	Boeing B.707-328	Waterkloof
Central Flying School (CFS)	Pilatus PC 7 Mk II Astra	Langebaanweg
85 Advanced Flying School (AFS)	Atlas Impala I & II	Hoedspruit
86 Multi-Engined Flying School	Casa 212 Aviocar, C-47TP	Bloemspruit
87 Helicopter Flying School (HFS)	Alouette III, Atlas Oryx	Bloemspruit
SAAF Test & Development Centre	Pilatus PBN 2A Islander	Bredasdorp

(MAP)

90

APPENDIX III: SAAF Indigenous Aircraft Names, Markings, Codes and Serials.

Bosbok	Atlas-built Aermacchi AM-3CM
Cheetah E	Atlas up-graded Dassault Mirage III
Cheetah C/D	Atlas up-graded IAI Kfir C 10
Impala I	Atlas-built Aermacchi MB.326M (two-seat)
Impala II	Atlas-built Aermacchi MB 326K (single-seat)
Kudu	Atlas-built Aermacchi AM-3C4M
Kukri	Amscor AAM (Kukri, is the curved knife of the Gurka Soldier)
Mercurius	Mercury the messenger - HS 125-400B
Oryx	Atlas-built AS-330S2 Puma
Rooivalk	Atlas CSH-2 Attack helicopter.

Bostok, Impala and Kudu are varieties of Antelope. Rooivalk = Red Kestrel.

The SAAF is divided into three territorial area commands, with both Southern (coastal patrol*)* and Western Command having *helicopters and transports* assigned and Air Space Control Command, combat aircraft *(interceptors, fighters, fighter-bombers and light attack planes)*, and Training Command with *fixed and rotary-wing trainers*. The operational unit is the squadron.

SAAF national markings changed after WW II from a UK-type roundel (see rear cover), to a similar insignia but with a centre red springbok. After South Africa became a Republic in 1961, the change was made to a plan view of a fort (blue star), with a blue centre with a gold springbok, subsequently in the mid-1990s the centre gold springbok was supplanted with a gold eagle. At times in the interest of maintaining anonymity on clandestine and highly secret operations during the Bush Wars and on counter-insurgency operations the airplanes were devoid of markings. Cessna Caravan Is and other types used on light transport, observation and communications duties were painted in 'civil' livery and carried civil (ZS-) registrations. Albeit, 'cheat' lines etc., appeared in air force blue !

Sgt C Crouse

No. 41 Squadrons Cessna Caravan Is were operated in the Bush War years in 'civilian' livery with civil (ZS-) registrations. Subsequently superceded with military serials *(ad astra)*

Civil registrations included:

ZS- LPE	HS 125 *Mercurius*	SAAF 04
ZS-JBA	HS 125 *Mercurius*	SAAF 05
ZS-JIH	HS 125 *Mercurius*	SAAF 06
ZS-LPF	HS 125 *Mercurius*	SAAF 07
ZS-LME	HS-125 *Mercurius*	

| ZS-CAQ | Dassault Falcon 50 | (Government aircraft) No. 21 (VIP) Squadron |
| ZS-CAS | Dassault Falcon 50 | (Government aircraft) No. 21 (VIP) Squadron |

ZS-JLU	Piper PA 27 Aztec	(captured Angolan airplane)
ZS-JLW	Piper PA 27 Aztec	(captured Angolan airplane)
ZS-JPV	Beech Queen Air	

| ZS-KEJ | Beech Queen Air | |

ZS-LAY	Beech 200C Super King Air	
ZS-LNT	Beech 200C Super King Air	
ZS-LNV	Beech 200C Super King Air	
ZS-LXS	Beech 200C Super King Air	
ZS-LOF	Beech 200C Super King Air	
ZS-LPR	Vickers Viscount Srs 781D	SAAF 150 (Government aircraft - wfu)
ZS-LIG	Cessna 550 Citation	(VIP No. 21 Squadron)
ZS-NAN	Dassault Falcon 900	(Government aircraft - wfu)
ZS-LYR	Cessna Caravan I	
ZS-LZS	Cessna Caravan I	
ZS-MEF	Cessna Caravan I	
ZS-MEG	Cessna Caravan I	
ZS-MEH	Cessna Caravan I	
ZS-MHJ	Cessna Caravan I	
ZS-MHL	Cessna Caravan I	
ZS-MHU	Cessna Caravan I	
ZS-MLM	Cessna Caravan I	
ZS-MLP	Cessna Caravan I	
ZS-MLR	Cessna Caravan I	
ZS-MLT	Cessna Caravan I	

| ZS-JMA | Swearingen Merlin | |
| ZS-JLZ | Swearingen Merlin | |

No. 41 Squadron Cessna Caravan Is subsequently carry military serials but remain in 'civilian' livery *(ad astra)*

Post-war, SAAF Harvards kept their old World War II military serials (7001-7799), as did the piston-engined Douglas C-47 Dakota transports (6801-6884). In 1971, five ex-South African Airways Dakotas ceded back to the SAAF were allocated 'old' serials 6885-6889. Five Douglas DC 4 carried 6901-6905 serials and the three Douglas C-54A serials 6906, 6907 and 6908.

A revised new serial range ran from 01 to nearly 1100, since extended to -2000 and beyond for the locally-assembled Pilatus PC 7 II 'Astra' trainers. Type serials appear not to have been allocated in chronological order. When this did occur, it was usually purely accidental as in the case of the Dassault Mirage III follow-on orders. Extra large high-viz serials using black lettering on a yellow background were displayed on the Harvard trainer fleet, placed centrally on the fuselage immediately below the cockpit. Brief details of types and serials are detailed:

01-07   HS-125-400B *Mercurius* (04, 05, 06, 07 used civil ZS-LPE, ZS-JBA, ZS-JIH, ZS-LPF plus additional airplane ZS-LME.

No. 21 (VIP) Squadrons HS.125-400Bs were the only airplanes of the type equipped to launch underwing rockets
(Hawker Siddeley Aviation Ltd)

Serial	Type
15-22	Aerospatiale Alouette II
23-76	Aerospatiale Aloutte III
77-80	Not used
81-97	Westland Wasp HAS I (Plus 1 Westland Scout - did not carry SAAF civil or Mil serial)
101-109	D.H. Dove
101-120	Aerospatiale Alouette III (serials 101-109 re-allocations)
120-121	D.H. Heron Srs 2B
121-190	SA 330 Puma (serials 189 and 190 used civil ZS-HNK and ZSHNJ respectively)
200 series	D.H. Vampire FB.52 and T.55/1 re-allocated Mirage F.1s.
200-215	Dassault Mirage F.1CZ
216-247	Dassault Mirage F.1AZ
300 series	North American P-51 Mustang (re-allocated)
301-316	SA321 Super Frelon
331-339	Transall C-160Z
-342	Atlas Cheetah C
350-383	Canadair CL 13B Sabre 6
388-	Atlas Cheetah C 354, 368, 369, 370, 372 representative (re-allocations)

401-407	Lockheed C-130 Hercules
408-410	Not used
411-426	Blackburn Buccaneers
427-442	Not used
451-456	EE Canberra B(I) Mk 12
457-459	EE Canberra T Mk 4
460-610	Atlas Impala I
600 series	NA F86F Sabre (20 aircraft loaned by USAF- Korea)
611-647	Aerospatiale Aloette III
710-754	Cessna C.185A/D/E
800-815	Dassault Mirage IIICZ
816-818	Dassault Mirage IIIBZ
819-834	Dassault Mirage IIIEZ
835-838	Dassault Mirage IIIRZ
839-841	Dassault Mirage IIIDZ
842	Dassault Mirage IIIEZ
843-853	Dassault Mirage IIID2Z
854-857	Dassault Mirage IIIR2Z
858-862	Atlas Cheetah D ex-IDF/AF Kfir 1
881-900	Piaggio P166S Albatross
920-959	Atlas AM 3C Bosbok
960-999	Atlas C-4M Kudu
1000-1099	Atlas Impala II
1200-1250	AS-330S2 Atlas Oryx
1701-1715	Short Sunderland IV
1716-1723	Avro Shackleton MR 3
-2029	Pilatus PC 7 II (representative serial)
-3012	Cessna Caravan Is (representative serial)

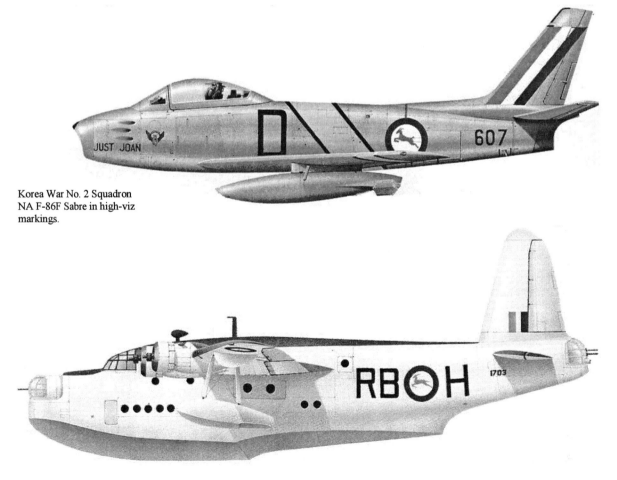

Korea War No. 2 Squadron
NA F-86F Sabre in high-viz
markings.

No. 35 Squadron Short Sunderland GR.IV serial 1703 circa 1946, still carries British 'RB' military identification code!

APPENDIX IV: ATLAS AVIATION, A Division of DENEL (Pty) Ltd.

Recognising the need to establish its own airplane manufacturing facility in South Africa, the Atlas Aircraft Corporation of South Africa was founded in 1963, to set up such a facility at Jan Smuts Airport. The first type selected to be licence-built was the Italian Viper 11-engined Aermacchi MB 326M unarmed two-seat jet trainer in 1966. The first sixteen airplanes were imported from Italy in completely knocked down kit form for assembly in South Africa and serial 460 was assembled at Ysterplatt Air Force Base in May 1966 and handed to the SAAF on 3 June that year. The remaining fifteen were assembled by Atlas Aircraft Corporation. The next twenty airplanes also arrived in kit form for assembly but with a number of locally manufactured components. However, from serial 506 onwards the Impala I, as it was named, was manufactured locally with only limited imported components. The last Impala I was handed over to the SAAF on 29 August 1974, when production of this model ceased with a total of 151 built.

Maj F Naudé   An Atlas Aircraft Corporation silver-finish Atlas Impala I dual-seat trainer high up in the mountains *(ad astra)*

Production switched to the improved single-seat operational trainer and light attack model Impala II based on the Aermacchi MB 326K with a Viper 20 Mk 540 engine. South African manufacture began with the assembly of seven airplanes supplied in kit form from Italy, the first of which were handed over to the SAAF on 22 April, 1974.

Camouflaged single-seat Impala II with long-range tanks and underwing stores. *(ad astra)*

The Atlas AS-330S2 Oryx was born out of the SAAF's requirement to replace its SA 330 Pumas with a Super Puma type airplane. One was converted from an ordinary Puma (serial 177), which was re-serialled 1250 as the prototype. The Oryx fuselage was manufactured on the Puma production line in Romania and sent to South Africa where the remainder of the helicopter was built and assembled by Atlas at Jan Smuts. By July 1995, serials 1200-1242 had been delivered to equip four SAAF squadrons: No.17 at Swartkop, No.19 at Louis Trichardt, No.22 at Ysterplaat and No.15 at Durban. From serial 1235 onwards the Oryx was equipped to accept flotation equipment.

In 1981, Atlas Aviation started their research for a light attack helicopter (Alpha XH-1) using many South African produced components and sub-assemblies of the Aerospatiale SA 316B Alouette III. The Alpha prototype flew on 3 February 1985, with a new tandem cockpit, and an almost new fuselage, fitted with a rugged tail-sitter landing gear.

Development of the Rooivalk attack helicopter began in late 1984. Atlas converted two SA 330 Pumas to act as test beds for the programme, both airplanes to take on very different development tasks. The first XTP-1 flew in 1986 and undertook stub-wing development, and sub-system concepts and evaluation. XTP-2 was used to evaluate the weapons fit and to test fire the 'turreted' 20mm GA-1 cannon and other stores including unguided rocket clusters, beam-riding anti-tank missiles and heat seeking air-to-air missiles. This allowed the Atlas engineers to concentrate on the design of the first prototype Rooivalk airplane known as the XDM powered by two Topaz locally-upgraded Turbomecca Makila locally-manufactured engines. Three prototype Rooivalk were built, with a fourth doubling as the first series airplane. The first prototype (XDM) was rolled out on the 15 January 1990, and made its first flight on 11 February the same year. For the test programme XDM was configured with the pilot in the rear seat and the front seat occupied by a flight test engineer.

The ending of the war in South West Africa (Namibia) and subsequent defence cuts removed the SAAF's need for the helicopter, the government withdrew funding and the programme was temporarily halted late in 1990. Nonetheless, the project was restarted as a company funded venture with a number of overseas buyers showing interest in the design. The second prototype advanced demonstration model (ADM) made its first flight during the second quarter of 1992. Based on experiences with the XDM, the second prototype featured some redesign of the tail area but was also more representative of the series Rooivalk, having for the first time integrated airframe, full avionics and weapons systems. As such, this machine had the pilot in the front cockpit and the weapons systems operator (WSO) in the rear.

Atlas Aviation CSH-2 (Combat Support Helicopter) Advance Demonstration Model (ADM) (ZU-AHC).
(Atlas Aviation)

Following a demonstration of the helicopters full operational capabilities in March 1993, the SAAF placed an order for four machines in October that year. Increased to sixteen in mid-March 1994. Later the civil registered (ZU-AHC), ADM appeared at the 1994 Farnborough Air Show, Hants, in the UK and later the same year, it was displayed at the Middle Wallop International Helicopter Air and Trade Show. Following these appearances in the United Kingdom, partnered by Marshall of Cambridge, Denel/Atlas submitted an unsolicited bid for the British Army attack helicopter requirement at this time, but later was eliminated. The UK opting for the AgustaWestland-assembled Boeing WAH-64 Apache Longbow instead. By early 1995, the two prototype machines had flown over 600 hours between them. Over 400 by XDM and over 200 by ADM. The third prototype, the engineering development model (EDM) with sponsors for ammunition storage and additional avionics flew in May 1996. Subsequently further budgetary constraints saw the SAAF order reduced to just twelve Combat Support Helicopters CSH-2 Rooivalks and these now equip No.16 Squadron at Bloemspruit.

Design of an home-grown turboprop trainer, started in September 1985, by government research agency Aerotek, initially as a technology demonstrator (Aerotek Ovid) for composites. Then known simply as the "New Generation Trainer"(NGT) turboprop trainer, it formed the basis of an Atlas prototype turboprop trainer (Aerotek 8000) that made its first flight on 29 April 1991. Proposed later that year as a Harvard replacement, the SAAF displayed little interest in the airplane, instead choosing the Swiss Pilatus PC 7 II as its replacement trainer. Not being selected, Atlas decided to market the trainer for export as the 'Ace'.

Atlas Aviation turboprop 'Ace' trainer receiving attention at Farnborough in the UK, circa 1994. *(author)*

Following civil registration (ZU-AHE) in September 1993, 'Ace' made its foreign debut at Dubai International Air Show in October, and later flew at Farnborough in the UK. However, back in South Africa, on the 14 February 1995, it was badly damaged in a wheels-up landing and did not fly again. A proposal to build a second prototype was abandoned and the project scrapped.

Having changed its name to Atlas Aviation on 1 April, 1992, Atlas later become a division of Denel (Pty) Ltd. In July 1995, Atlas established a store for withdrawn SAAF airplanes at Jan Smuts. At that time around 23 SA 330 Puma, two Rooivalk test airplanes (serials 189 and 190) and 14 Aerospatiale Alouette IIIs were stored there. As well as two inherited Bophuthatswana Air Force (serials T200 and T240) Aloutte IIIS and Venda Defence Force Air Wing (serial VDF-001) Alouette III withdrawn from SAAF use.

The dual-seat BAe Hawk Mk 120 with an uprated Rolls-Royce Adour 951 engine is the subject of an off-set agreement for local manufacture by Denel/Atlas Aircraft Pty Ltd. Following production and the first flight of the first Mk 120 by BAE Systems at its Brough facility in the North of England in the UK, in October, 2003. Local deliveries by Atlas are scheduled to commence in 2005 continuing until 2009. The first Atlas produced batch to include nine airplanes to replace the Cheetah Ds with No.2 Squadron Training Flight at Louis Trichardt AFB.

BAe Systems Hawk LIFT 100 carried South African national colours on its demonstration tour in 1995. Subsequently the SAAF ordered twenty-four of the more powerful Mk. 102s. *(BAe Systems)*

Other major upgrades and manufacturing projects undertaken by the Atlas Aircraft Corporation in the years of the international embargo against the former South African regime, were the Mirage III, Cheetah E conversions and the Israeli Kfir, Cheetah D and C conversions and the re-configuration of the Aermacchi AL60 light transport for use by the SAAF in the Bush Wars. At the same time a number of air-to-air missiles were developed specifically for use by the Mirage F.1s in the Angolan War. Details of these important projects have already been given in the main text.

No. 2 Squadron combat-capable Cheetah D with silver underwing tanks *(T. Shia)*

The improved tranche 2/3 BAe/Saab JAS 39 Gripen has an uprated Volvo Flygmotor RM12 engine, improved computers and can carry more weapons, with its retractable inflight refuelling probe affording greater range. The SAAF has 19 s/s and 9 d/s on order *(author)*

APPENDIX V: C-47TP Turbo-Daks

Towards the end of the 1990s, realising there was a need to bolster its transport assets and there was little chance of satisfying its needs on the international market due to the UN sanctions still in place, the SAAF decided to modernise and re-engine the fleet of forty or more Douglas C-47 Dakotas it had on inventory. Although a WW II design, as the basic airframe was sound and its ruggedness and suitability for local conditions was well proven, it was decided a more powerful turboprop variant would be acceptable for SAAF use.

Meanwhile, in the United States, the American Basler Company, at Oshkosh, had already completed a number of turboprop conversions for the USAF, the airplanes intended for use in South America by air forces already operating the piston-engined civil DC 3 and military C-47 Dakota, the airplanes supplied under the Military Aid Program (MAP). The original Pratt & Whitney R-1830 engines were replaced by the lighter and more powerful Pratt & Whitney Canada PT6A-65 turboprop engines. This bestowed the ageing transport with increased payload and range, the only penalty being a fuselage stretch was needed to maintain the correct centre-of-gravity (C of G). Known as the Basler 67, the prototype made its maiden flight in July 1989, and although various DC 3 re-engining projects had been muted in the past, the Basler Turbo project was a resounding success. Following the initial delivery a steady trickle of airplanes left the Oshkosh facility, mainly for military customers in Central and South America.

The SAAF conversion first appeared in 1988, and looked similar to the Basler 67 ! Subsequently, a conversion licence was obtained from the American company Aero Modifications Inc., for what became known as the C-47TP Super Dakota. At the same time, the UK company, Hunting Aviation set up a PT6 engine maintenance and overall facility at Rand Airport. Two airplane production lines were set up, one at Snake Valley AFS (since absorbed into Swartkop AFB) and at Ysterplaat under Project 'Felstone' to convert the ageing C-47s, the work being undertaken by SAAF personnel rather than contracted civil companies. The conversion was planned to take about six weeks per airplane at an estimated cost of $1.7 million each. A major milestone in the four year programme was achieved on 26 August 1991, at Ysterplaat near Cape Town, when C-47TP serial 58, formerly C-47B-35-K serial 6858 was rolled out.

The 'new' SAAF Dakota incorporated, a fuselage 'plug' aft of the cockpit of 1 metre (3 ft 3.25 ins) to maintain the C of G; the WW II-vintage cockpit had been modernised with new avionics designed by Ruetech Systems; updated hydraulics and electrics; and new non-slip steel floor with freight tie-downs had been added. During modernisation/conversion all the airframes were stripped to the bare metal and corrosion treated, giving the airframe 'zero-rating'. The new powerplants demanded minor changes to the airplanes ailerons, elevators and rudder in accordance with the improved performance afforded. During SAAF acceptance trials, the airplane exhibited an increase in range of more than 500 nm to 1,517 nm and an increase in maximum cruising speed by 35 knots to 185 knots true air speed (TAS).

The first C-47TP entered SAAF service with No.35 Squadron at D.F. Malan Airport, Cape Town, (the unit on detachment from Ysterplaat), in 1992, and subsequent deliveries were made to No. 44 Squadron at Waterkloof and 86 Multi-Engined Flying Training School at Bloemspruit. On completion of the programme it is believed some 32 to 39 C-47TPs were delivered, although accurate figures are not available. The 'new' airplanes used for training and light transport duties, with others used for target-towing and maritime patrol work. Later a dedicated Maritime patrol variant was produced.

At the same time as plans for the transport plane conversions were put forward, Ruetech Systems were already undertaking a feasibility study into the possibility of producing a dedicated Dakleton Maritime Patrol variant with a patrol range of 4,800 km. With No.35 Squadron already reporting favourably on their four "makeshift" piston-engined C-47 Dakota maritime planes and having received tentative approval from the powers that be, Reutech moved into the concept phase in October 1992. This involved the design of a specialised integrated maritime mission system and this was installed in a trials airplane fitted with nose-mounted FLIR ball and cabin windows deleted, which began flight test in September, 1995.

Subsequently a proposal to re-introduce a number of Transall C-160Z modified for the maritime patrol role was dropped. Instead by the end of 1995, the SAAF had ordered eight dedicated maritime C-47TP Turbo Daks for delivery between 1997 and 1999. The first fully-equipped airplane flew in 1997, with the trials programme undertaken between April and October that year, at the SAAF Test and Development Centre at Bredasdorp and with No.35 Squadron at Ysterplaat AFB. The programme concluded in 1999. Currently (2003) all eight remain in service with No.35 Squadron at D.F. Malan AFB Cape Town, IAP.

Prototype Ruetech Systems maritime patrol C-47TP Dakleton in 'maritime' colour scheme *(Ruetech)*

SAAF plans to re-introduce the C-160Z Transall in the maritime role were subsequently abandoned. *(ad astra)*

101

A Douglas C-47 Dakota tactical transport, C.208 Caravan I and a No. 35 Squadron
Maritime C-47 Dakota occupy the flight line at D.F. Malan AB *(ad astra)*

A prestine Ruetech Systems maritime C-47TP 'Super' Dak stands ready on No. 35 Squadrons dispersal.

The C-47's old 'front office' has undergone almost total revision when compared with the new C-47TP Super Dak's below

APPENDIX VI: SAAF Museum Inventory.

Many Lockheed Model 18 Lodestar civil airliners were pressed into military service early in WWII. As were a number of SAA airplanes. Example shown is the SAAF Museums ZS-ATL. *(SAAF Museum)*

Type	Serial	(c/n)	Date acquired	Remarks
Aerospatiale Alouette II	22	(1280)	March 1983	
Atlas Impala I	460	(102/633)	Nov 1992	
Atlas Impala I	501	(165/6396/A26)		
Atlas AM3C Bosbok	920	(2001)		
Atlas AM3C Bosbok	959	(2040)		
SA 330C Puma	123	(1030)	1992	ex- No. 19 Sqdn
SA 321 Super Frelon	309	(129)	Feb 1991	ex- No. 15 Sqdn
SA 321 Super Frelon	314	(140)	Feb 1991	ex- No. 15 Sqdn
Atlas C4M Kudu	969	(19)	Nov 1990	ex- AFS Snake Valley
Atlas C4M Kudu	972	(22)	April 1992	ex- No. 41 Sqdn
Atlas C4M Kudu	987	(29)	Nov 1990	ex- No. 41 Sqdn
Atlas XH-1 Alpha			Jun 1992	Atlas research airplane

Type	Serial	(c/n)	Date acquired	Remarks
Auster J/1	ZS-BML		April 1991	incomplete airframe
Auster J/1	ZS-DGF		May 1985	fuselage only
Auster J/1	ZS-BKW		Jan 1982	ex- AFS Snake Vallley. Derelict, used for diamond smuggling attempt
Airspeed Oxford 1	G-AITF		Feb 1987	ex- RAF Museum
Avro Anson 1	4437		Jan 1974	restored
Avro Anson 1			Jan 1976	ex- AFS Snake Valley crash site recovery
Avro Anson 1	4588		1975	Ex- AFS Snake Valley. airframe only
Avro Shackleton MR.3	1716	(1526)	Dec 1984	ex- No. 35 Sqdn - airworthy, was crash landed in the desert en-route UK 1994.
Avro Shackleton MR.3	1719	(1529)	1993	ex- No. 35 Sqdn
Avro Shackleton MR.3	1721	(1531)	Dec 1984	ex- No.35 Sqdn
Avro Shackleton MR.3	1722	(1522)	Dec 1991	ex- No.35 Sqdn
Beech C-45G-BH	ZS-EOG		Dec 1978	ex- AFS Snake Valley
Beech C-45H-BH	N57948		Jul 1979	ex- AFS Snake Valley
Beech C-45H-BH	A2-AOS		Dec 1976	ex- AFS Snake Valley
Bristol Beaufighter X	BF-10		May 1983	ex- *Museo do Ar Portugal*
Canadair Sabre 6	361	(1470)	April 1976	ex- 15 Air Depot Snake Valley
Canadair Sabre 6	367	(1476)	July 1982	ex- 15 Air Depot Snake Valley
Canadair Sabre 6	372	(1481)	Feb 1987	ex- 15 Air Depot Snake Valley
Dassault Mirage IIICZ	800	(149)		Airworthy airplane
Dassault Mirage IIICZ	804	(157)	Oct 1990	ex- No. 2 Sqdn
Dassault Mirage IIICZ	813	(178)		SA War Museum
Dassault Mirage IIIBZ	816	(228)	Oct 1990	ex- No. 2 Sqdn
Dassault Mirage IIIBZ	818	(230)		ex- No. 2 Sqdn
Dassault Mirage IIIRZ	835	(1F1A)	Oct 1990	ex- No. 2 Sqdn
Dassault Mirage IIIRZ	837	(3F3A)		ex- No. 2 Sqdn
Dassault Mirage IIIRZ	838	(4F4A)		ex- No. 2 Sqdn
Dassault Mirage IIIR2Z	857		Oct 1990	ex- No. 2 Sqdn

Type	Serial	(c/n)	Date acquired	Remarks
Douglas C-47A-10-DK	6832	(12478)		ex- No.35 Sqdn
Douglas C-47 Dakota	6859	(12586)		ex- 86 MEFTS
Douglas C-47 Dakota (2)				
Douglas DC-4-1009	6902 ZS-BMF	(43155/67)		ex- No. 44 Sqdn
Douglas AD-4N Skyraider	TR-KFQ		Nov 1985	ex- Gabon AF
Dornier Do 27Q-1	ZS-CMA		Aug 1983	
Dornier Do 27Q-4	5430		May 1979	
D.H. Vampire FB.5	205		Mar 1991	ex- Fort Beaufort
D.H. Vampire FB.5	208		Mar 1988	ex- Fort Klapperkop
D.H. Vampire FB.52	219		1975	ex- SoTT, Lyttleton
D.H. Vampire T.55/1	221		Aug 1976	ex- RhoAF
D.H. Vampire T55/1	222		Mar 1979	ex- RhoAF
D.H. Vampire FB.52	229		Jul 1974	Atlas Aviation - fomerly used for apprentice training. Loaned
D.H. Vampire FB.52	241		Aug 1991	ex- Bloemfontein War Museum
D.H. Vampire T.11/2	R4032		Sep 1984	ex- RhoAF
D.H. Vampire T.55/1a	257		Feb 1985	airworthy airplane
D.H. Vampire T.55/2	271		Aug 1980	ex- RhoAF
D.H. Vampire T.55/2	276		Feb 1985	airworthy airplane
D.H. Vampire T.55/2	277		Nov 1978	
D.H. Tiger Moth II	2341		1975	
D.H. Tiger Moth II	ZS-EUV		Feb 1980	fuselage
D.H. Hornet Moth	2007		Jan 1981	
DHC Chipmunk T.10	WG354		Jul 1980	ex- RAF
Edgar Percival E.P.9	XM797		Jan 1981	ex- British Army evalution airplane
EoN Olympia	ZS-GAV		Mar 1982	
EE Canberra T Mk 4	457 (WJ991)	(71543)	Dec 1991	ex- No.12 Sqdn SAAF (ex-RAF)
EE Canberra T Mk 4	458 (WJ864)	(71332)	Dec 1991	ex- No.12 Sqdn SAAF (ex-RAF)
Fairchild Argus III	KK476		Jun 1982	ex- RAF
Fairchild Argus III	VP-YNF		Oct 1980	ex- playground Harare, Zimbabwe ex- AFS Snake Valley. Derelict
Fieseler Fi 156C-7 Storch	VD+TD		May 1975	ex- Luftwaffe
Frankfort TG-1A	ZS-GIB		Oct 1984	
HS Buccaneer S.50	414	(SA4 17)	April 1991	ex- No. 24 Sqdn
HS Buccaneer S.50	416	(SA6 19)	1991	ex- No. 24 Sqdn
HS Buccaneer S.50	421	(SA11 40)	April 1991	ex- No. 24 Sqdn
HS Buccaneer S.50	422	(SA12 42)		SA War Museum

Type	Serial (c/n)	Date acquired	Remarks
Lockheed Lodestar	ZS-ATL	April 1983	
Lockheed Ventura II	6075	Oct 1978	
Lockheed Ventura II	6112	Feb 1976	ex- AFS Snake Valley
Lockheed Venture II	6120	Feb 1976	ex- AFS Snake Valley
Lockheed Ventura V	6447	Nov 1988	ex- SAA Jan Smuts
Lockheed Ventura V	6487	Nov 1973	
Lockheed Ventura V	6498	Nov 1988	ex- SAA Jan Smuts
Mikoyan MiG-21bis	C-340	1991	ex- Angolan Air Force. Forced landed in SWA (Namibia) damaged.
Miles Gemini 1A	ZS-BRV	Jul 1979	salvaged parts only
NAA Harvard III	7506	April 1990	ex- Stilfontein
NAA Harvard III	7570	1975	Atlas Aviation - fomerly used for apprentice training. Loaned
NAA P-51D-20-NA Mustang	325	Nov 1987	ex- Dominican AF
On Mark Marksman	ZS-CVD	Feb 1982	ex- AFS Snake Valley (B-26C Invader ex-USAAF 44-34567)
Patchen TSC-2 Explorer	2000	April 1987	
Percival Prentice T.1	VS609	Feb 1974	ex- RAF
Percival Provost T.52	137	Sep 1983	ex- Air Scouts, Bulawayo, Zimbabwe
Piaggio P.166S Albatross	881 (447)		ex- No. 27 Sqdn
Piaggio P.166S Albatross	896 (448)	Oct 1991	ex- No. 27 Sqdn
Piper Cherokee 140	2004	Dec 1978	ex- No.10 Air Depot. Wreck.
Piper Cherokee 140	ZS-IEL	May 1981	ex- Benoni. Parts used for 2004
Sikorsky S-51	A-1 (51-102)	Feb 1978	ex- No. 17 Sqdn
Sikorsky S-55 (HAS.22)	A-5 actually A-4 (55-959)	May 1984	
Sikorsky S-55 (HAS.22)	WV203	Dec 1976	ex- Autair, Grand Central. (former RAF)
Sikorsky S-55 (HAS.22)	WV204	May 1980	ex- Henlock Ltd, Kew. (former RAF)
Supermarine Spitfire IX	5518	Mar 1979	ex- Waterkloof AB
Taylorcraft BL-65		Feb 1978	fuselage frame only
Westland Wasp HAS.1	93 (F9755)	1991	ex- No. 22 Sqdn
Westland Wasp HAS.1	95	1991	ex- No. 22 Sqdn
Westland Wasp HAS.1	96	Mar 1991	ex- No. 22 Sqdn
Westland Scout AH. 1	ZS-HHA	Aug 1989	ex- RAF serial XT562
Westland Scout	BSP-1 (F9619)	Mar 1989	Ex- Bahrain Police -SAAF. Never carried SAAF or South African civil registration
C-160 Transall	337 (Z4)		

North American Harvard Inkwazi serial 7001 built from spares! Traditionally was personal mount of CFS Commandant. *(ad astra)*

F/sgt D Rowles One of the SAAF Museum's D.H. Vampire T.55/2 (serial 277) at a very wet Swartkop Museum hardstanding. This airplane displayed with the Atlas Impala II 'Gannet' at the SAAF's 75th Anniversary Airshow held at Waterkloof AFB in 1995. *(ad astra)*

Bibliography & Sources

	Aviation Magazines, various
Chant Christopher	Air Forces of the World, Brian Trodd Pub House Ltd., London, 1990.
Dancey Peter	Author's personal archives
Halley James J	The Squadrons of the Royal Air Force & Commonwealth 1918-1988. Air-Britain (Historians) Ltd. Tonbridge, Kent, UK, 1988.
Jane's	All the World's Aircraft 1945. HarperCollins Publishers, London, 1994.
Jane's	Aircraft Upgrades 1995-96, Jane's Information Group Ltd, Surrey, UK 1995.
Lewis Peter	Squadron Histories, Putnam, London, 1959.
Lloyd Mark	The Guinness book of Helicopter Facts and Feats, Guinness Pub. London 1993.
Pearcy Arthur	Lend-Lease Aircraft in WW II. Airlife, Shrewsbury, UK. 1996.
Wilson Ian	Who's Who in Aviation and Spaceflight, Pocket Reference Books, Bournemouth, UK, 1996.

Acknowledgements:

My special thanks goes to the SAAF Public Affairs staff and for their 'ad astra' photo editions bequeathed to the author at the IAT (International Air Tattoo) in 1995, at RAF Fairford, Glous, UK. Photographs sourced from the 'ad astra' photo editions, are accredited. All other pictures are from the authors collection, the T. Shia collection, or other sources as anotated. Thanks also goes to Atlas Aviation, a Division of Denel (Pty) Ltd, for various product information, technical details, airplane illustrations (front and rear covers), and photographs as anotated.

Acknowledgement and my sincere thanks also goes to the SAAF Media Liaison and Public Relations Departments, the Friends of the SAAF Museum, SAP Air Wing, SA Broadcasting Corp TV and Radio, and the following writers and correspondents, Maj Johann Rankin, Michael Hamence, Roland van Maarseveen, Frédéric Lert, Gérard Gaudin, Soutie v.d. Merwe and Al J Venter and any other persons I have been unable to contact in the process of researching the information for the book.

ADDENDUM

In a special ceremony at the SAAF's Test Flight and Development Centre (TFDC) at Bredasdorp on 4 February 2004, the first BAe Hawk Mk 120 (serial 250) for the air arm was received for the first phase of the types flight test programme. First flown at BAE's Warton aerodrome in the UK on 2 October 2003, the airplane will be based at the Bredasdorp test facility for development flights, and testing of the engine and avionics systems. The airplane was dismantled and air-freighted from the UK to South Africa on an Antonov An-22 transport on 17 October. The remaining 23 Hawks will be assembled by Denel from kits supplied by BAE Systems.

Operational Hawks will be based at the re-named Makhado AFB (formerly Louis Trichardt AFB) - the change of name resulting from the township of Louis Trichardt itself being re-named Makhado.